the Parrot
Problem Solver

Barbara Heidenreich

T.F.H. Publications, Inc.
One TFH Plaza
Third and Union Avenues
Neptune City, NJ 07753

This book has been published with the intent to provide accurate and authoritative information in regard to the subject matter within. While every precaution has been taken in preparation of this book, the author and publisher expressly disclaim responsibility for any errors, omissions, or adverse effects arising from the use or application of the information contained herein. The techniques and suggestions are used at the reader's discretion and are not to be considered a substitute for veterinary care. If you suspect a medical problem consult your veterinarian.

Printed and bound in China
06 07 08 09   3 5 7 9 8 6 4 2

Library of Congress Cataloging-in-Publication Data
Heidenreich, Barbara.
The parrot problem solver : finding solutions to aggressive behavior / Barbara Heidenreich.
p. cm.
Includes bibliographical references and index.
ISBN 0-7938-0562-7 (alk. paper)
1.   Parrots-Training. 2. Parrots-Behavior. I. Title.
SF473.P3H45 2008
636.6'865–dc22
2005003442

Dedicated to the care and well-being of companion animals for over 50 years.
www.tfh.com

Table of Contents

Acknowledgments

I would like to thank the following people for their continued support. First, I would like to thank my parents for supporting and nurturing my career with animals. All those trips to zoos, horse farms, pet stores, the woods, etc. meant a lot to me and certainly shaped my future. As always, I need to thank my good friends, Lea and Adam Czyzweski, for the emotional support, intellectual stimulation, inspiration, and of course, editing skills. Thank you to my good friends, Terry and San Debrow, for more than I can possibly say. Their generosity is immeasurable. I'd like to send a big thank you to the friends made at zoos and animal facilities around the world while working on this book. This includes friends at Earth Rangers, Dallas World Aquarium, AfriCam Safari, and more. The experiences gained there go way beyond simple professional goals. Special thanks go to Jerry, Michael, Linda and Jennifer at J & M Aviaries for being so supportive in general and allowing me to photograph their birds. To Julie Murad and the staff at Gabriel Foundation, I thank you so much for welcoming me and opening the door to so many opportunities, not to mention the good work you all do for parrots. Thank you to the students and faculty in the Department of Behavior Analysis at the University of North Texas at Denton for the opportunity to observe their research projects, especially to Nicole Dorey and Jesus Rosales-Ruiz. Thank you to Dr. Thomas Edling for creating the opportunity for this book to exist. To Dr. Suan Friedman, I am so very thankful to learn from you and I admire the tremendous positive impact you have made on the parrot community. And, as always, thank you to the animals who have enriched my life beyond compare.

Introduction

Parrots are amazing creatures. They can be strikingly beautiful. They can be famously entertaining. They demonstrate a remarkable intelligence. They can form powerful bonds with the people in their lives. Experiencing the intense devotion of a companion parrot just might be the ultimate form of flattery. A bonded parrot may preen your hair, gently nibble on your ear, generously share his undigested food with you, and defend your honor by viciously attacking any other suitors. If your parrot is a talker, he might even say, "I love you" several times a day. How many animals—or even family members for that matter—live up to the bonded parrot's high standard of devotion?

With such an incredible capacity to captivate our hearts, it is no wonder many people now have parrots in their homes. However, lurking beneath the surface of that adorable, fluffy baby parrot is, at heart, an animal that is essentially genetically the same as his wild cousins. Although most companion parrots available today are the result of captive breeding, there are many similarities in the behavior of those individuals that live in our homes and those that live in the wild.

When given proper attention and training, a parrot, such as this umbrella cockatoo can become an incredibly devoted and affectionate pet.

This is an important concept to consider. By understanding natural behavior of parrots in the wild, we have a better opportunity to understand the behavior of the parrots in our homes. Looking at wild parrot behavior can help us to understand why parrots bond so strongly with people. Why do they regurgitate for us? (This is certainly not a sign of love in human terms!) Why do they attack other people when they come too close to you and your bird? Why do they mimic sounds? And so on.

This book aims to explore the mysteries behind one type of natural behavior that can turn even the smallest cockatiel into a ferocious feathered beast. That behavior is aggression. How can it be that your

As a behavioral consultant and professional animal trainer, I have experienced many interesting stories and words of advice from various sources on how to deal with bird behavior. Look for these special sections for examples and perhaps alternative ways to look at common behavior scenarios.

most devoted companion can sometimes become a biting machine? Or perhaps you graciously offered to rescue a neglected parrot only to find out that your kind attempt to make friends with this bird only got you bloody fingers instead of the companion you had hoped.

Aggression is a very real, observable phenomenon in parrots. Like a great deal of behavior, it follows some very specific patterns. In other words, often we can use the science of behavior to predict and prevent aggression. We will explore the observable physical characteristics of aggression. What might be surprising is just how small these physical characteristics can be. We will also examine how aggression is created and perpetuated by the choices we make when interacting with our birds. This will require learning to read and interpret bird body language that indicates aggressive behavior. Aggression also is motivated by a number of different things. For example, sometimes your snuggly cockatoo might bite you when he doesn't want to return to his cage, or he may grind his beak on the bars of the cage when a stranger approaches his cage. These two types of aggression are motivated by different circumstances. Learning how to diminish

Although most of the parrots in the US and Europe are hatched and raised in captivity, they are not really domesticated. They are genetically and behaviorally the same as their wild ancestors.

Aggression in parrots is no joke! Parrots have sharp beaks and strong jaw muscles. Even the smaller species can draw blood, while larger species like scarlet macaws can cause serious damage.

aggression in these situations requires us to identify the type of aggression first before we consider an appropriate method to eliminate it.

Most people reading this book have probably already experienced an aggressive parrot and are looking for solutions. We will explore a variety of methods and practices that can help reduce and/or eliminate aggressive behavior in parrots. These methods are all based on positive interactions and positive reinforcement. This book will not recommend the use of punishment (other than a "time-out"), force, or other negative experiences to deal with aggression.

We will also consider how some traditional methods fail to diminish or eliminate aggression and some common pitfalls that also prevent us from achieving success. Of course, we will also explore methods you can utilize to reduce and/or eliminate aggressive behavior without sacrificing a loving relationship with your companion parrot. It is my hope that the following pages will provide a deeper insight into the workings of aggression. While it is not usually fun to be on the receiving end of aggression, it is a most fascinating subject. I hope you find the journey enlightening.

Behavior

Behavior. What a fascinating subject! It is all around us. Every day people (and animals) do or don't do things based on the very same principles. For example, what motivates us to get out of bed and go to work? Why do we put on a seatbelt when we get in the car? Why do we answer the phone when it rings? Or don't answer it when we think it is a telemarketer? Why do we have companion parrots in our homes? And why does our companion parrot scream at 6:00 in the morning?

Believe it or not, the answers to all these questions have something in common—the science of applied behavior analysis. Behavior became an important area of study in the late 1800s and early 1900s. B. F. Skinner is one of the leading early behaviorists. He and his colleagues set out to answer those questions and tried to decipher the mechanisms that govern behavior. What is so amazing is that some very precise patterns began to emerge. In some ways these mechanisms seem like common sense to us. After all, we are "behaving" everyday. Humans can see how specific behavior patterns can create certain results. However, Skinner took these common sense ideas and gave structure

Remember that your bird has what he considers a good reason for the things he does. This includes behaviors you consider unpleasant, like screaming.

and foundation to this burgeoning area of study. Thanks to Skinner and other scientists, we are now armed with a wealth of information to help us understand how behavior works. Not only does this information help us understand human behavior, but it also can give us insight into the behavior of animals.

Therefore, our journey into understanding aggression begins with a look at some of the important principles of behavior. When interacting with your companion parrot it is helpful to reflect on these concepts and note how these theories may affect behavior. Remember, these all can be applied to humans as well.

Animals Do Things for a Reason

Look again at all the questions at the beginning of this section. It is not too difficult to provide answers for most of them.

Scarlet Macaws are"nippy"?

Many times our experiences with a species lead us to describe them in general terms. Scarlet macaws are nippy, Amazon parrots are hormonal, and cockatoos are cuddly. In many cases we do see trends that lead to these statements. However, it also important to remember not to jump to these conclusions before thoroughly examining the motivation for the behaviors in question. I had the privilege of working with 12 young (just weaned) scarlet macaws. This was an excellent opportunity to test the theory that scarlet macaws are nippy. I have trained a number of parrots over the years using positive reinforcement. The techniques I have learned rarely, if ever, result in a parrot that seeks out opportunities to bite. Therefore, if I could produce the same results with these young scarlet macaws, then perhaps what was making scarlet macaws nippy was the training and handling techniques and not some innate characteristic of the species. Lo and behold, we ended up with 12 scarlet macaws that behaved much like any other macaw species I had trained. It was a good lesson that perhaps the reputation of scarlet macaws was not earned, but rather learned.

Although scarlet macaws have a reputation for being nippy birds, the author used positive training methods when raising 12 young ones. Those scarlet macaws grew up to be no more nippy than other macaws.

- What motivates us to get out of bed and go to work? A paycheck, the satisfaction of doing a good job.
- Why do we put on a seatbelt when we get in the car? To avoid a ticket, to save our lives, to avoid the buzzing noise.
- Why do we answer the phone when it rings? It could be a loved one, perhaps someone needs you.
- Why don't we answer the phone when we think it is a telemarketer? To avoid having to say no, to avoid being interrupted.
- Why do we have companion parrots in our homes? We enjoy their company, they talk, they can be affectionate, and they are beautiful.
- Why does our companion parrot scream at 6:00 in the morning? To indicate well-being, due to instinctual drive, to make a contact call with you.

It seems obvious, but often we forget that actions are a result of motivation. Sometimes we don't have an easy explanation for why an

Always reward your bird for good behavior. Food is not the only possible reward that will motivate a companion parrot. Many parrots enjoy attention, affection, and praise, and those actions make effective rewards.

animal or person did what they did. This does not mean there was not motivation created by the resulting consequencesf past experiences. It just means we need to dig a little deeper to determine the motivation. Sometimes people will say a parrot bit them for no reason. But if we remember that animals do things for a reason, we can then start asking ourselves questions that can help us get on a path to solving the problem. It is easy to get in the habit of looking for the motivation for behavior. Simply start observing your bird's—or even family members'—behavior and try to answer the question, "Why did he or she just do that and what outcome did it produce?"

Ignore Bad Behavior and Reward Good Behavior

If you want a behavior to go away, do not reinforce it. If you want a behavior to continue, reinforce it. Again this seems like common sense. However, it is astonishing how easy it is to forget this simple concept. The following example demonstrates how easy it is to get confused.

Once while working on an animal training consulting project, I accompanied a group while they presented a program about parrots to school children. An instructor spoke about parrot conservation while an umbrella cockatoo perched on a stand off to his side. The cockatoo bounced emphatically on the perch hoping to attract the instructor's attention. Finally the bird leapt off the perch and landed on the ground. The instructor immediately ran over to the cockatoo and scooped him off of the ground. On the walk back to the perch, the instructor lavished the cockatoo with kisses and cuddles. He then placed the bird on the perch, verbally instructed him to remain there and then continued his lecture. Shortly thereafter the bird leapt off the perch again. I watched the process repeat itself over and over for the duration of the talk. The children loved it!

Obviously in this situation the cockatoo enjoyed the attention he received when scooped up off of the ground. When the bird was returned to the perch, all the attention disappeared. In essence the instructor did exactly the opposite of what he needed to do to keep the bird sitting calmly on the perch. He rewarded the behavior of jumping onto the floor with kisses and attention, and ignored the behavior of

This Catalina macaw likes being up on his companion's shoulder and does not want to come down. From a parrot's point of view, being forcibly removed from a companion's shoulder is negative reinforcement.

sitting calmly on the perch. This is an easy mistake to make. However, it demonstrated the importance of remembering to ignore bad behavior and reward good behavior.

Negative Reinforcement and Positive Reinforcement

Negative and positive reinforcement are deceptive. This may seem like a strange comment. However, the deceptive component has to do with our human interpretation of negative and positive. Applied behavior analyst Dr. Susan Freidman says the basic definition of negative reinforcement states that the removal of a stimulus following a behavior will maintain or increase the frequency of the behavior. Another name for negative reinforcement is escape/avoidance training. Negative reinforcers tend to be aversive or unpleasant to the bird. To avoid negative reinforcers, learners often only work to the level

Forced Flapping

In this day and age of super-sizing, we have also created some super-sized parrots! Exercise is often recommended as a way to fight parrot pudge. However, sometimes it is a challenge to get those feathers in motion. One method sometimes recommended to get those wings flapping is to place your bird on your hand and then drop your hand. Instinct does kick in and the wings come out and flap to maintain balance and perhaps protect the bird from a perceived crash to the ground. However, is the bird doing this by force or choice? Does the bird have to or want to? While some birds do learn to accept this practice, many birds appear to be quite uncomfortable. This does not mean your bird is destined to be a perch potato. Consider other options for exercise, such as foraging trees, scattering or hiding healthy food items, novel enrichment items, large enclosures, climbing options, swings, active play sessions, etc. Your bird can look forward to exercising by providing positive reinforcement as the end result of each action.

necessary to avoid them. Positive reinforcement is the presentation of a stimulus that also serves to maintain or increase the frequency of the behavior. Another name for positive reinforcement is reward training. However Positive reinforcers tend to be valued or pleasant experiences for the bird. What is missing is a clearer definition of what it is the *animal* likes or does not like. For example, negative reinforcement can be very, very small. Most birds in the wild do not like to sit with the wind blowing against their tail feathers. To avoid the negative reinforcement of the wind on the tail, the bird will turn to face into the wind. Another example is when a person slips a finger under a parrot's toe and lifts the bird up off of the perch. Again this action is very tiny, but technically it is negative reinforcement. The point is that negative

Whenever you want your bird to perform a behavior, you should ask yourself, "Does my parrot want to do this?" If you are using positive reinforcement, your parrot will usually be eager to perform.

and positive is in the eye of the beholder. In other words, it is important to determine what the bird sees as negative or positive.

Why does this matter? Both methods can produce desired behavior, right? Yes, negative and positive reinforcement both work to teach an animal a behavior. The drawback of negative reinforcement is that something the animal perceives as negative can be associated with the handler. This can be detrimental to developing the best relationship possible with the animal. Also, an animal trained with negative reinforcement only works to the level required to escape the negative reinforcement. The behavior most likely can also be obtained using positive reinforcement. In some cases it may take longer to train using positive reinforcement, but the end result is an animal that looks forward to the interaction and is typically anxious to do more to receive the positive reinforcement.

On one consultation I had the pleasure of working with two skunks and a mink that could not be released back to the wild. These animals were part of the wildlife rehabilitation facility's education program.

One of the skunks and the mink had a history of aggressive behavior. Because of this, their futures as education animals were in question. Using positive reinforcement we began training simple behaviors such as touching a stick with their noses and entering a kennel voluntarily. This eventually evolved into training other behaviors such as digging, swimming (for the mink), climbing, etc. However, the most rewarding part of the process was watching the attitude of the animals change. Animals that would usually be sleeping, aggressive, or not interested in us at all suddenly could not wait to interact with us. Have you ever seen a skunk with a "smile" on its face? It was deeply rewarding.

An easy way to determine whether you are using positive or negative reinforcement is, as bird trainer Steve Martin often suggests, to ask the question, "Does the animal *want* to do what I ask or does it have to?" Another way to look at it is to ask yourself, "Is this force or choice?" If the animal has to or is forced to do the behavior, the mechanism at work is negative reinforcement. If the animal has the choice to participate or not, or it actually wants to participate, the mechanism at work is positive reinforcement. Aim to use positive reinforcement as much as possible and you can expect an exceptional relationship based on trust between you and your companion parrot.

Chapter 2

Parrot Behavior in the Wild
and What We Can Learn From It

I love dogs. I love being able to pet them all over, let them lick my face, chase a ball, and take a walk with me. I also love how most dogs are quick to make friends with a stranger (human or dog). I love parrots, too. I love how my parrot will let me scratch his head; he preens my eyebrows, plays with a bell, and will sit with me while I work on the computer. He is not so quick to make new friends, but having four out of five qualities is not too bad.

While both types of animals can be phenomenal companions, the truth is they are very different. Their differences do not necessarily arise from training but rather from genetics. Why is it that my parrot would prefer I touch only his head and not his entire body? Why does my bird preen my eyebrows instead of lick my face like the dog? And why is he so finicky about new birds or people? Quite simply, many parrot species in our homes are genetically the same as parrots in the wild. Therefore, many things they do are based on instincts that are useful for survival in the wild. For example, we know preening feathers is important for keeping them in good condition. Parrots cannot reach the feathers on their own heads. Therefore they are usually open to letting other

Since parrots cannot preen the feathers on their own heads, they will allow their mates to preen this area. This may be why parrots often are more at ease with humans petting their heads than the rest of their bodies.

parrots preen the feathers on their heads. There also appears to be an important social component to allowing another bird to preen head feathers.

Parrots also do many other natural behaviors that make sense for survival, but can be frustrating to a companion parrot owner. For example, bonding to one person in the household makes sense if you are a parrot. In the wild parrots typically form strong pair bonds and drive other suitors away. The aggression that is exhibited is particularly intense near the nest site and surrounding territory. It makes it easier to understand why your sweet parrot may become as territorial as a well-trained guard dog once sexual maturity hits.

It also explains why making new friends is usually not quite the carefree experience as it is with dogs. Many parrots typically only hang out with their "friends" when it is wise for survival. For example, when birds are foraging or roosting, they can be more vulnerable to predators. Having a large group means many eyes can be on the lookout for

Wild parrots form strong pair bonds and will drive other birds away from their nest. In the home, this can translate into a companion parrot bonding with one person and being aggressive to other household members.

predators. It can also mean mass confusion for a predator when the flock springs into flight. In homes, food is abundant and usually predators are not lurking about. Therefore, the only friend a companion parrot may need is the one he perceives as his mate. This is not to say parrots cannot learn to interact with other people. They certainly can if those interactions are positively reinforcing to the parrot.

There are many behaviors that can be explained by observing and studying parrot behavior in the wild, including many aggressive behaviors. Keep this in mind when your bird does something that you find puzzling. Sometimes the answer lies in natural behavior.

Let's explore behavior of parrots in the wild a little deeper. While studies of parrots in the wild are relatively few, a good comprehensive project can be very enlightening. One such project is the study of the decline of the Puerto Rican parrot. *The Parrots of Luquillo: Natural History and Conservation of the Puerto Rican Parrot* by Noel Snyder, James Wiley, and Cameron Kepler (1987) is a book dedicated to exploring the decline of this species as well as conservation efforts. In addition it provides an excellent overview of daily life for the Puerto Rican parrot. While this study focuses on one species of parrot, the authors note that similar research demonstrates the same pattern of behavior exists for a number of parrot genera. The following information reflects what can be learned about parrot behavior in our homes by studying parrot behavior in the wild.

The italicized material is paraphrased from *The Parrots of Luquillo*. See the bibliography for a complete citation.

A Typical Morning For a Wild Parrot

Most will agree that morning begins at sunrise. Just like in our homes, the day in the wild usually begins quietly with birds slowly beginning to stir. As the sun rises birds may stretch one wing to one side, followed by the other. This might be followed by some quiet preening. Some small sounds may be made but in the wild the parrots are generally quiet as they make sure everything is safe.

However the silence doesn't last too long! Shortly after the sun has fully risen, birds vocalize and burst into flight. Pairs of parrots make short flights to different perches, squawking all the while. Chosen perches are usually at the very tops of trees, giving the birds a perfect view of their neighborhood, other parrots, and potential predators. In general they are very alert and aware of their surroundings. The squawking helps define territories and other parrots appear to recognize the boundaries.

Parrots have been recorded screaming in the morning from 1 minute up to 150 minutes. It has also been noted that species that are more gregarious have a greater diversity of calls. In addition, vocalizations have been shown to be extremely important in pair bonding. At some point the vocalizations stop for the morning and the parrots head off to forage.

What can we learn from this?

Parrots are naturally vocal and active early in the morning (from 1 minute to 150 minutes).

Vocalizations are important for social behavior and pair bonding.

Vocalizations are used to indicate territories and appear to be

Vocalizing in the morning is a natural behavior for parrots. These vocalizations are important for defining territories and maintaining pair bonds. Companion parrots often feel the need to make noise in the morning.

respected by other parrots.

Feeding and Foraging Behaviors

Sometime between 6:00 a.m. and 9:00 a.m. parrots fly to feeding areas. Usually they follow the same flight paths to feeding areas. Some birds have been known to fly great distances to acquire food—even miles.

While eating, birds are usually very quiet. Some species focus on a particular food item. Others have been found to eat a wide variety of food items. If food is abundant, parrots are more likely to take one or two bites out of an item and leave the rest uneaten. They contribute more to the mess by rubbing their beaks on nearby branches after feeding. Of course, some food still remains encrusted on the beak. Besides being messy eaters, parrots are also slow eaters. That does not stop them from filling up quickly. In some species, parrots can fill their crops completely in well under an hour.

Another interesting observation is that parrots have been seen in the wild favoring a particular foot for holding food. One study shows that the left foot was preferred to hold food in 94 percent of the observations recorded.

Predators are a threat every parrot must consider. When feeding, a parrot is quite often distracted and vulnerable to attack. Because of this it is likely that many feeding behaviors are practiced in a way that helps protect birds from predators. For example, parrots normally feed quietly and in groups. Another interesting antipredator behavior is the use of "sentinels." Sentinels remain perched high with good visibility of the surrounding area while other birds eat. These birds scan the area for predators. One alarm call from a sentinel can send the entire flock of foraging birds into flight. The mass confusion of a group of birds in flight can foil a potential predator's attempt at a meal. A sentinel is not necessarily a parrot with any innate distinction. It is any member of the group that for the moment carries the role of scanning for predators while other members of the group feed.

What can we learn from this?

Parrots usually forage from 6:00 a.m. to 9:00 a.m.

Parrots may go long distances to forage.

Parrots are messy eaters.

Parrots are usually quiet when eating.

In the home or in the forest, parrots are messy eaters. A parrot owner must come to accept this mess as part of life with her pet.

Parrots usually like to be in pairs or larger groups for feeding.

Parrots tend to favor one foot to use for holding food.

Parrots eat a wide variety of food items in the wild.

Parrots sometimes use a sentinel to stand guard while the flock is feeding.

A Typical Afternoon for a Wild Parrot

Usually after foraging, parrots in the wild enter a resting phase. In the resting phase parrots can be found preening, feather fluffing, sleeping or just generally being relatively inactive.

As the day progresses parrots may enter a particularly deep state of rest. During this time parrots appears to enter an even more inactive phase. In the wild, parrots in this state are often difficult to find. They will nestle far into the bushy parts of trees. They will ruffle their feathers and tuck their beaks over the backs. A parrot in this deep state of rest typically remains tucked up in a ball, even when activity may be occurring nearby. It takes a serious threat for a parrot to rouse from this afternoon nap. Encounters that might normally cause a cautious parrot to burst into flight may only cause a bird to open its eyes, yawn or stretch at this time of day. Researchers theorize that during the midday there are many pairs of parrots hidden throughout the forest quietly digesting their breakfast.

Starting around 3:00 p.m. the parrots begin to stir from their afternoon naps. Vocalizations begin to increase in volume and birds begin to move around. All this activity signals the start of the second feeding period. The second feeding period usually begins between 3:30 p.m. and 4:30 p.m. Birds continue to feed as late as 7:00 p.m. After feeding, birds return to their roosting locations. Before calling it a night, parrots expand some energy calling and flying throughout their territories.

What can we learn from this?

Parrots like to rest during the midday.

This state of rest can be very deep.

Parrots tend to become vocal and active again in the late afternoon.

Parrots usually feed again in the late afternoon anywhere from 4:00p.m. to 7:00p.m.

Parrots tend to be vocal and active one more time before roosting for the night.

Parrots typically become less active in the afternoon. This hyacinth macaw might spend the afternoon preening, sleeping, scratching, or just hanging out. Later in the day, parrots will become active again and enter a second feeding period.

A Typical Evening for a Wild Parrot

After calling and flying about, parrots choose their roosting locations for the evening. Some parrot species roost in large conspicuous flocks, while others can be very secretive about their locations. Either strategy can be effective against predators. Large flocks allow for more individuals that might notice a predator and sound the alarm. An alarm call can send an entire flock into the air creating confusion for the potential predator. Pairs that bury themselves deep in the foliage utilize camouflage to go undetected in the night.

Very rarely do parrots fly at night by choice. In other words, parrots are very careful to arrive at roosting locations before the sun has set. Some observations of parrots in the wild suggest that parrots demonstrate *tremendous difficulty navigating in the darkness. Therefore, it makes sense that arriving home before nightfall would be a wise survival strategy. Parrots have been known to fly at night if startled or frightened by something. This often results in a burst of flight that seems to have no particular direction other than to escape the suspected danger.*

What can we learn from this?

Parrots become vocal again when returning to roost.

Large groups of parrots are more vocal than small groups.

Parrots like to go to roost before the sun has set completely.

Apparently, some species do not see well at night.

Parrots do not fly at night unless frightened.

Reproductive Behavior of Wild Parrots

The previous information focused on the behavior of a parrot during non-breeding season. It is important to keep in mind that breeding behavior has a great influence on the daily activities of a parrot. We will now explore reproductive behavior of the parrots and again look for similarities in the behavior of parrots in the wild and the home.

Research shows that many parrot species do not normally change mates from year to year. However, if a parrot's mate dies or is lost for another reason, the lone parrot will quickly try to acquire another mate. This makes good survival sense. A parrot is unlikely to have reproductive success if he dwells on the mate that is lost.

Despite this smart survival strategy, parrots have also been observed making choices that do not appear to be quite as intelligent. For example, one parrot was observed attempting to copulate with his mate while facing the wrong way! This same parrot was also observed feeding his mate, quite normally, via regurgitation. The female bobbed her head to solicit more food. But in response, the male attempted to masturbate on a tree branch. This masturbation took place while the female, who was quite receptive to mate, was sitting beside the male. Perhaps this particular male was not well-schooled in the art of smart reproductive strategies.

Many birds demonstrate particular behaviors involved with reproduction that can be quite fascinating. Parrots are no exception. Some species will bow in unison. Large macaws will mimic body postures such as wing and head positions. Parrots with large patches of bare skin may flush to

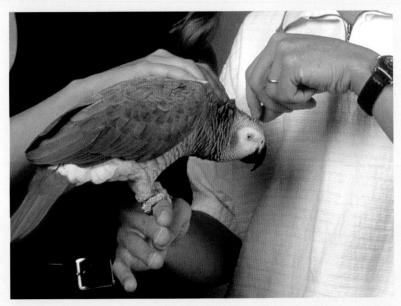

Paired parrots engage in frequent bouts of mutual preening called allopreening. Companion parrots often look to their owners to provide this kind of attention. Parrots sometimes become ill when deprived of normal social interactions.

a red color. Some parrots exhibit a behavior called bowing; the bird bends his body forward as if taking a bow. Many times behaviors such as these are followed by several minutes of soft mumbling and attempted mutual preening (also called allopreening*).*

Some species of parrots are incredibly social. This is especially true of gregarious species such as lovebirds. Dilger (1960) found that captives of the more social Agapornis *species (commonly referred to as lovebirds) became ill and died if they were deprived of normal social interactions, such as mutual preening, when in the presence of other parrots. Saunders (1974) similarly emphasized the potential importance of allopreening in the behavioral repertoire of the white-tailed black cockatoo. Social interactions can be very important for parrots.*

What can we learn from this?

Parrots usually form a strong pair bond with one individual.

Parrots will sometimes switch that bond to another individual rapidly, especially if the original partner is lost.

Parrots attempt copulation with their mates (sometimes quite unsuccessfully!).

Parrots will beg for food from their mates by bobbing their heads.

Parrots will offer food to their mates via regurgitation.

Parrots will sometimes masturbate.

Parrots may also exhibit specific pair bonding behavior, such as bowing.

Mutual preening can be very important to the physical and behavioral health of some parrot species.

Territorial Behavior of Wild Parrots

Although birds will defend territories to some degree at other times of the year, intense territorial behavior has been seen primarily around nest sites and typically only around breeding season. Because most birds tend to forage outside of their nesting territories, it has been concluded that the aggressive behavior is not likely about protecting food sources. In addition, parrots that may fight over a nest site may forage together side by side without a quarrel. Territory size can vary tremendously. Usually competition with neighbors can effect the size of the territory. More competition usually indicates a smaller territory.

Territorial displays of aggression usually begin with vocalizations. If the threatening bird is very close to the nest site, sometimes the resident parrots choose to be very quiet, perhaps in hopes that the other bird will not discover the nest site. If the invading bird is persistent, eventually the resident parrots will respond. If an intruder is far away, the pair may quickly fly to the highest vantage point in their territory to identify the intruders. The display may end with a series of calls back and forth; however, it also may escalate. Some species of birds have been observed in face-to-face confrontations, screaming at the tops of their lungs.

As the breeding season approaches it is not uncommon for quarrels to become more intense, even leading to physical combat. Birds use their beaks to lunge at opponents' heads and feet. If aggression is particularly high, birds will become entwined in battle. The devotion to the fight is so intense that birds will tumble to the ground locked in battle. Loud vocalizations often accompany the fight. In between attacks pairs may strenuously preen each other and also bite chunks out of branches. The most intense displays and

Parrots exhibit intense territorial aggression around their nesting sites, sometimes developing into serious physical fights. Both male and female parrots engage in the defense of the nest and other territory.

battles are frequently seen between birds with neighboring territories. These fights can be so intense that predators such as hawks have been known to successfully capture a parrot engrossed in a battle. In addition, humans have been able to hand catch parrots that are so distracted by territorial aggression. Such drive may indicate certain parts of the brain that govern the fight or flight response are in overdrive! In other words, a parrot's brain may be on autopilot as it remains focused on the battle for territory.

Parrots are selective as to what they consider a true threat to their territory. For example, a juvenile bird may be allowed to pass through the territory while an adult may not. Parrots appear to be quite adept at identifying individuals. And it is possible they are able to do this based only on vocalizations. Parrots are also careful not to waste energy on territorial behavior when it is not necessary. It has been noted that parrots in locations with few neighboring pairs may rarely vocalize. If another parrot does enter the territory both male and female will make their presence known and defend the territory. The drive can be so strong that the female will leave eggs or young unattended.

What can we learn from this?

Parrots can be extremely territorial about an area they perceive to be a nest site.

Parrots will defend territories that can be quite small or quite large.

Parrots can seriously hurt invaders of their territories.

Parrots will usually vocalize before attacking an intruder to their territory.

Parrots will lunge at an intruder's head and feet.

Parrots can become locked in a battle with an opponent and be unaware of activities outside of the battle.

Territorial parrots are likely to be more aggressive with other adults seeking nest sites than they would be with juveniles.

The drive to defend a territory is so strong a female will leave eggs or young unattended to protect her territory.

Territories can be defended year round, but usually more so during breeding season.

Parrots may displace aggression by strenuous mutual preening and branch chewing in a territorial encounter.

In some cases, territorial aggression becomes so severe, parrots will leave eggs or hatchlings unattended while they attempt to drive off intruding birds.

Parrots may be able to recognize individuals based on vocalizations. Parrots may choose to fight only with individuals they perceive as a threat.

Other Interesting Behaviors of Wild Parrots
Chewing Objects Near the Nest Site

It comes as no surprise that parrots in the wild also exhibit a variety of behaviors that involve chewing. Around the nest site, parrots have been observed chewing on branches and vines near the nest hole. It is thought that fresh chew marks may indicate to others that the site is taken. It may also be a signal amongst the pair that one or the other is ready to begin work on the nest. Finally, it may be an expression of displaced aggression or frustration perhaps in association with territorial bouts.

Chewing Inside the Nest

A great deal of chewing activity occurs within the actual nest hole. This can serve a variety of purposes. Chewing may expand the nest hole; it may provide a soft substrate for egg laying; and it also may help dry out the cavity and create a suitable environment for incubation.

Rapid Scratching Inside the Nest Site

Another activity also seen in some parrots in the home is rapid scratching on a substrate. In the wild this activity seems to be connected to preparing the nest site for egg laying.

What can we learn from this?

Parrots chew on objects near the nest site.

Parrots chew in the nest site.

Parrots may chew on something to indicate possession.

Parrots may chew on something to indicate that they are fit.

Parrots may chew on something to displace an emotional state such as frustration or fear.

Parrots will use their feet to rapidly scratch and rearrange nest substrate.

Very little published information exists on the detailed activities of parrots in the wild. *The Parrots of Luquillo* is an excellent resource that describes in great detail the daily behavioral patterns of wild Puerto

Chewing is a normal and natural behavior for parrots. In the wild, they chew on a variety of objects, including branches and vines near the nest. This may be a form of territorial marking.

Rican parrots. For me, every page provided new insight into the behavior exhibited by parrots in our homes. It again reinforced that parrots in our homes are not far removed behaviorally from those in the wild. *The Parrots of Luquillo* focuses on one particular species. As referenced here and from personal experience, it appears many of the behavior elements described apply to other species as well.

Few studies of Psittaciformes (parrots and cockatoos) have been conducted in the wild, and these studies consider only 8 percent of the psittaciform species. Such a lack of information is of particular concern as parrots and cockatoos have become the most endangered order of birds in the world during the last few decades (Masello and Quillfeldt, 2002). There are a number of excellent groups working on conservation of parrots in the wild. Think how much more we can learn about these amazing creatures by supporting field research. The back of this book contains some information on conservation projects focused on parrot species. By getting involved with preserving parrots in the wild, we can also indirectly help understand companion parrots in our homes.

Parrots Come From the Rainforest, Right?

We often think of parrots as tropical rainforest species. While it is true many parrot species live in rainforests, many are also found in several other types of habitats, and some do not live in tropical rainforests at all. Species such as hyacinth macaws, green-winged macaws, blue and gold macaws, jenday conures, and blue-fronted Amazon parrots are found in the rainforest, but these species are also found thriving in arid locations. These areas can get quite chilly at night. In addition some parrots, such as keas, naturally live in areas where snow is a normal occurrence. Pick up a book on parrot natural history and discover the conditions in the wild for your species of parrot. Even better, take an eco-tour and see the species in the wild!

Blue and gold macaws and other colorful parrots symbolize the tropical rainforest to many people. However, parrots come from a variety of habitats, including savannahs, scrublands, and some temperate habitats.

Chapter 3

Pitfalls to Avoid
When Looking at Parrot Behavior

It was once suggested to me that people are obsessed with companion parrots because they make a great substitute for a child. Perhaps on some level this is true. However, parrots are not children. Parrots are parrots. This may seem like a silly statement to make because it is quite obvious. On the other hand, it is a helpful concept to consider when looking at parrot behavior. Sometimes our human interpretations of behavior lead us to make erroneous conclusions about our parrots. For example, how many times have companion parrot owners been bit and had their feelings hurt? Often, this leads to conclusions that the bird hates the owners, is evil, mean, nasty, deceptive, calculating and so on. Many times the birds are given up for placement, which doesn't really address the biting issue.

It is difficult for people to do, but putting the emotions aside can help solve the problem. Instead of saying, "My bird hates me," ask yourself, "What did I just do that my bird did not like?" Instead of saying, "My bird is just mean," ask yourself, "What would be his motivation for biting in this moment?" The answer could relate to natural behavior in the wild. Was his territory invaded? It could also be that he learned biting will stop you from doing something he does not like. Was he being forced to step up on the hand? There are many scenarios to consider. The next section will describe different situations that can cause aggressive behavior. The important thing is to think like a parrot and not like a human when you are trying to evaluate parrot behavior.

Animal training has a very long history. Some of the history is not always pleasant. Many of the "traditional" methods for training animals still persist. I remember being told as a child if the dog had an accident in the house, we were to push his nose into the pile, say "No," and put the dog outside. I also remember family members yelling for the dog to come and then hitting him with a rolled up newspaper for taking too long to respond. Experience and research shows us now that these methods are not nearly as effective as kinder, gentler ways of teaching your dog what you want. I wonder how many dog owners still use those methods? Probably more than I want to know about. The point is that just because that is the way it had been done in the past, doesn't mean

These fairy penguins voluntarily enter their transport crate. Because they were trained with positive reinforcement, the penguins are eager to enter the crate and receive their reward.

Super Size Me!

Have you ever seen a bird with a bowl of food that looks to weigh twice as much as the bird? Overfeeding seems to be a fairly common practice. Unfortunately, it is probably not too healthy for the bird. A bird that has a food bowl in front of it, with much more food than it can eat in a day, typically only eats out the most desirable or palatable items. Usually this means the more healthful and nutritional items are left behind. Determine what your bird is eating by weighing the diet before you feed. Twenty-four hours later, weigh what is left. It is best to use small increments of measure, such as grams if possible. You may be surprised by how little a parrot may eat during a day. This doesn't mean you should not feed your bird until he or she is satiated. Instead, it means to closely evaluate exactly what your bird is eating so that he or she may enjoy a healthy diet and life. There are wonderful recipes for breads and mixes that help finicky birds learn to enjoy healthful foods.

companion pet owners should continue to use those methods today.

Some methods from the past are still in use today do produce good results. However, it is also important to look at the mechanism in which those methods work. For example, people can learn not to touch a hot stove by accidentally touching a hot stove one time. This would be a very cruel way to train this behavior, but it probably would work. When considering methods to use, it is important to determine if that method has other drawbacks or consequences. In most cases there are other ways to get desired behavior that do not have to be harsh or detrimental. Here is a common parrot example: Sometimes companion parrots may need to go to the veterinarian or other destinations. Using a kennel for transport can be quite convenient, as it fits readily in the car. For some,

In zoo situations, animals are now being trained to calmly participate in their own health care. This Asian elephant has been trained to sit calmly while a veterinarian draws blood.

getting the bird to go in the kennel is a challenge. This may lead to the bird being grabbed with a towel and forced into the kennel. Obviously this method gets the desired result: the bird goes in the kennel. It is also possible to train the bird to voluntarily enter the kennel for positive reinforcement. This can be less stressful for everyone involved. The end result is the same, but the process is very different.

Currently there has been an increased trend in people wanting to learn how to get good behavior from their animals using positive reinforcement. Zoos use it to train animals to voluntarily participate in their own healthcare. Tigers sit calmly for blood draws; primates allow tuberculosis testing; pandas hold for x-rays; killer whales will even urinate on cue! Service dogs are trained to help disabled people. One horse expert even trained a miniature horse to do the same behaviors a Seeing Eye dog can do. Clicker training (positive reinforcement training in which the clicker lets the animal know he did something

Parrots Are as Smart as Two-Year-Old Children?

This is a very common statement. You hear it in animal presentations all the time. But is it accurate? On some levels, parrots do things that can be measured and compared to human behavior. However, parrots and humans are very different beings. Place a two-year-old human and a parrot side by side and it is hard to disagree. This, on the other hand, is not to say that parrots are not intelligent. On the contrary, they rank quite high in the animal world. They can also learn quite readily and via different mechanisms (such as classical conditioning, operant conditioning, modeling and more). Parrots are amazing, intelligent creatures! Perhaps a comparison to human intelligence is not necessary. Quite simply, parrots are smart—period.

It should come as no surprise that parrots are highly intelligent animals and are capable of learning complex behaviors. However, it's best to avoid comparing parrot intelligence to human intelligence, two very different species.

good) has become a buzzword in many animal communities. There are many dog training classes that no longer use choke collars and restraints to train but rather treats and rewards for a job well done. This trend has definitely found its way into the companion parrot community as well. No doubt it will continue to grow and evolve. In my opinion, this type of training can provide the solution to many companion parrot owners' pet behavior issues as well as offer an easy way to teach birds to do simple things like enter a kennel, allow a nail trim, get on a scale, wave, talk, etc.

While it is true we can do amazing things when we train animals using positive reinforcement, it is also important to remember that parrots are individuals. When performing free-flight bird shows, I received many offers from the public to take on their companion parrots. Many would describe the amazing things their birds knew how to do. But the truth is not all birds are destined to be in bird shows. Training with positive reinforcement does allow a great deal of progress, but each animal has limits. This also applies to companion parrots in the home. It is important to remember that not all parrots will learn to talk, allow you to cuddle with them, enjoy being touched, or interact with the entire household. It is rewarding when the excellent application of positive reinforcement and your bird's good genetics allow you to have all those qualities in one bird. But it is not always the case. Learning to accept that your conure may not be as cuddly as your friend's umbrella cockatoo need not be disappointing. Remember the other qualities your individual bird has that you find endearing.

Chapter 4

Aggression

Now that we have discussed some basics of behavior, it is time to narrow our focus and take a long look at aggression. As much as we may not want it to be true in our beloved parrots, aggression, on some levels, is a normal, natural behavior. Famous ethologist Konrad Lorenz noted that most animals have some degree of aggressive repertoire. Have you ever witnessed the undeniably distinctive aggressive strut and eye pinning exhibited by a territorial Amazon parrot? This is a very clear indication that its territory is off limits to all trespassers.

What is important to note is that some aggressive behavior is part of a parrot's survival strategy. Certainly it makes sense for a parrot to aggress in order to defend its nest site, mate, or offspring. Varying levels of aggressive behavior also enable a parrot to obtain food and other resources, and defend himself if necessary. In other words, aggression does serve a very important purpose in a parrot's natural history. In addition, a successful aggressive event can be quite reinforcing for the "winner" of the altercation. This teaches an individual that it is good to "win." Losing can result in many unwanted outcomes. A bird may lose

There are several different types of aggression, so a trainer or pet owner may need to employ different methods to correct aggressive behavior. Also, each bird is an individual and will respond in his own way.

his territory or resources, or have to endure unpleasant circumstances. Winners may look for more opportunities to be aggressive, while losers may avoid contact with an aggressor in the future.

Aggression can be classified into different categories based on the antecedents and consequences that contribute to the cause of aggressive behavior in those situations. These categorizations can be helpful to explore as a means to understand how and why aggressive behavior may be produced. The following section explores these categories in more detail.

Fear Aggression

When a parrot is afraid of something, his instinct is to go away from what he fears. However, companion parrots do not always have the opportunity to flee. Parrots in the home may be wing-clipped or confined within a cage. This in itself is not a problem in most cases. The challenge lies when a bird that is wing-clipped and/or is enclosed in his cage and is forced to deal with a fearful situation.

For example, picture a bird that has just arrived to a new home. Everyone in the household is excited and anxious to interact with the new addition. Having read in the latest parrot magazine that a bird should obey the "step up" command, one brave member of the family thrusts his hand into the cage and says, "Step up!" Instead of complying, the bird launches himself as far away from the hand as he can get. Now, the bird is scrunched in the corner of the cage. The determined family member persists and pushes his hand into the bird's body only to pull back a bloody finger. As a result everyone in the household is afraid, especially the bird.

What went wrong? Trying to force a fearful bird to interact with what he fears leaves a bird with little options. Birds present a variety of behaviors that indicate they are uncomfortable well before they bite out of fear. In essence all the small signals, such as darting looks, leaning

This cockatoo originally bit hands out of fear, and she learned that biting will make the scary hand go away. This is one way fear aggression gets reinforced and becomes learned aggression.

Stick Training: The Wrong Way

When a bird demonstrates he does not want to step up on a hand, quite often people will replace the hand with a stick. The reason is obvious: if a bird bites the stick, it doesn't hurt human flesh. This in turn, often results in a bird being chased around the cage until he acquiesces and gets on the stick. Over time, the bird learns to stop running away and get on the stick right away. This is because the bird learns that no matter what, the stick will continue to chase him until he steps up on it. This is how you train a bird to get on a stick using negative reinforcement. There are several drawbacks to training a bird to step on a stick with this method. One drawback is that to train the behavior the bird had to endure a very unpleasant experience. Furthermore, that unpleasant experience was associated with whoever was holding the stick. In some cases, birds learn to be extremely frightened of the stick and are traumatized to the point of fleeing whenever they see a stick. The good news is that stick training can be positive experience.

Learn how to train a parrot to step on a stick the right way in the next section.

Stepping up onto a stick is a useful behavior to teach your bird, but there is a right way and a wrong way to do it. If done properly, stick training can be a positive experience for you and your bird.

Stick Training: The Right Way

A parrot's beak can be very intimidating. Sometimes training a bird to step up onto a stick can be a good starting point to developing a relationship with a bird. It is important to train this behavior using positive reinforcement. Here are the steps to use with a bird that accepts treats from your hand.

1. Place the stick outside of the parrot's cage and leave it there for a few days. If the bird appears nervous, move the stick farther away until the bird relaxes. Each day move the stick closer to the cage as long as the bird is relaxed.

2. Slowly and gently bring an end of the stick up to the bars of the cage close to the bird. If the bird touches the stick with its beak, offer it a food reward. Allow the bird to explore the stick with its beak.

3. Slowly bring the stick into the cage and rest it on the perch where your bird is sitting, but away from your bird. If your bird is too frightened, go back to step two for a while. Hold a handful of treats on the side of the stick opposite to your bird.

4. If your bird makes any motion in the direction of the stick offer him a food reward.

5. Continue offering food rewards each time the bird moves closer to the stick.

6. If your bird touches the stick with his feet, offer him several food rewards.

7. Use the food treats to lure your bird to step onto the stick. Reinforce the bird for putting one foot onto the stick. Be sure to keep the stick very steady. Birds prefer a stable perch.

8. Once he has both feet on the stick, let him repeat the process of stepping on and off of the stick several times for positive reinforcement.

9. After the repetitions, you are ready to try moving the stick with the bird on it away from the perch. Remember to reward him when he gets on the stick. If the bird is nervous when the stick moves, let him go back to the perch. Repeat this until he begins to relax when on the perch and remain there longer.

10. When he is willing to stay there longer, then you can try bringing the bird out of the cage on the stick.

Training this behavior with positive reinforcement may take longer to train than the method of chasing the bird. Once it is trained, a bird will respond quite quickly because he looks forward to the stick—it means goodies are coming!

away, climbing or flying away are ways in which a bird says "no" with its body language. When a fearful bird bites, this is the bird's way of saying "NO!" as loud as he can. In many cases, the bite produces the desired result of causing the thing he fears to go away. This can then evolve into learned aggression.

Physical State-Induced Aggression

At one time or another all of us have been tired, injured, or ill. Sometimes our physical discomfort is so great that we snap at those who are only trying to help. Animals are no exception. This can often be a difficult type of aggression for companion parrots owners to experience. The desire to nurture and assist a loved parrot can be overwhelming, especially if that parrot is not feeling well.

An injured animal can be extremely aggressive when touched. Pain can sometimes elicit a reflex-like reaction of aggression. Medical treatment may require an animal to be physically examined. If your bird is experiencing illness or injury, rather than continue to interact with your bird, contact your avian veterinarian and seek assistance.

Even a well-behaved and sweet-tempered bird may become aggressive when ill or injured. This is one type of physical state-induced aggression.

Your veterinarian can accommodate your bird so that he or she is more comfortable. Keep in mind that some veterinarians have mobile practices and can make house calls if you have special circumstances that prevent you from getting your bird to the hospital.

Another physical state that can lead to "crankiness" is lack of sufficient rest. In the middle of the day it is not uncommon to see a parrot curled up with its beak tucked under its wing. At times a sleepy bird can be quite affectionate and receptive to gentle head scratches. However, some parrots prefer to be left alone when the yawning begins. Set yourself up for success by recognizing the signals that indicate your bird is not receptive to interacting at the moment.

Tired birds and birds that are ill or injured require companion parrot owners to proceed with caution and extra sensitivity. Asking for a behavior that may have previously been easy for a bird to perform, may now irritate a bird enough to cause aggression.

Redirected Aggression

There is a classic saying that claims we always hurt the ones we love. Apparently some of our companion parrots are familiar with this saying.

To illustrate redirected aggression, consider the following example: We have a woman spending some quality time with her companion parrot. Her husband arrives home and walks up behind her, not realizing Coco the cockatoo is nestled in her lap. Before the husband's lips reach his wife's cheek to greet her hello, Coco has made an impressive mark of his own on the wife's arm! What usually happens next is the bird is abruptly put back in the cage and the husband usually gets punished with a scolding.

In this scenario, Coco most likely was not comfortable having anyone else close to the person to whom he is bonded. Remember, parrots form very strong pair bonds in the wild. This bond can be easily transferred to a human counterpart. Although logic would say that Coco should try to bite the husband, in this example the bird chose to demonstrate his displeasure with the proximity of the husband by redirecting aggression on the closest thing available in that moment. In this case, it is the wife's arm. It does not mean the bird is less fond of the woman. Although it would be difficult to prove, I would venture to

One type of aggression is redirected aggression. This means the bird bites the nearest object or creature instead of directing that aggressive behavior toward the stimulus of the behavior.

guess the bird was hardly aware he was biting someone he loves. It is more likely Coco reacted almost spontaneously to the stimuli of the presence of the husband and also responded to his instinct that dictates he should not accept others close to his perceived mate.

Sometimes in this scenario it is theorized the bird is biting at his mate to encourage her to flee a perceived danger. I suspect this is not the case. When birds are afraid of something, the immediate response is to flee if at all possible. The few extra seconds it would take to bite his mate could mean life or death. A mate would quickly notice when her partner flees in fright and most likely will follow. Birds are very perceptive. It is unlikely it would take a bite to alert a bird that danger is present. A simple alert call would just as easily announce danger and can be done while hightailing it out of the area!

Territorial Aggression

Territorial aggression is a type of aggression that is often considered innate. This often means that certain circumstances trigger

This lovebird views the couch as her territory and is attempting to protect that territory with an aggressive display. Parrots usually do not exhibit territorial aggression until they become sexually mature.

physiological responses in parrots that can result in aggressive behavior. Many parrot species will experience hormonal changes that can result with age, when the seasons change, when nest box-like objects are in close proximity, or bonding behaviors (such as regurgitation) are encouraged. When hormonal status changes it may effect the readiness of an animal to respond aggressively because it effects the threshold of responsiveness to certain stimuli. These hormonal changes can also help support a strong drive to defend a territory.

Observation of parrots in the wild demonstrates that territorial aggression is quite natural. It is not exactly what most companion parrot owners had in mind when they acquired those adorable, baby parrots. Oftentimes, those babies mature and show a distinctly different, yet natural side to their personalities.

An image I find hard to forget is that of a woman trying to make "friends" with a small conure through the bars of the cage. The bird clung to the inside of the cage right in front of the woman's face. Clearly the bird was very interested in the woman. The woman, in her sweetest,

A finger poked through the bars of an unfamiliar bird's cage is likely to get bitten. This action can create aggressive behavior if the bird perceives the finger as an intruder to his territory.

most gentle voice was saying, "Hello, pretty birdie." At the same time she was poking her finger through the bars and trying to pet the head of the conure. The conure did his best to take a nice chunk of flesh out of her finger. And again, in her gentle voice the woman said "No, don't bite, little birdie" and continued to try to stroke the bird's head. This little conure was getting pretty worked up. But the woman persisted until finally, the conure succeeded in landing a strategically placed bite on the woman's well-meaning finger.

In this case the conure's extreme interest in the woman was probably due to some serious territorial aggression. The unfortunate woman thought it meant something else. Later we will discuss why trying to work through aggression by ignoring the aggression and continuing to work with the bird is not an effective strategy. In this case the woman, despite her good intentions, may have actually just made an enemy instead of a friend.

Possession Aggression

One of my favorite scenes from a very popular animated film about a lost fish illustrates possession aggression quite well. In one scene, the fish heroes of the film find themselves flopping around on a dock.

Nearby a large group of sea gulls perks up. One gull stretches his neck up and says, "Mine?" Suddenly every gull is racing towards the fish on the dock shouting, "Mine! Mine! Mine!" Chaos ensues and of course the heroes get away, but what an entertaining example of possession aggression (also called resource-guarding aggression).

While at certain times of the year, parrots will put forth considerable effort to ensure the survival of their young, they also demonstrate a strong preservation of self. Survival in the wild often means looking out for number one first. This means that selfishness, although not considered a virtue in humans, is probably a smart survival strategy for parrots. It is probably not unfair to assume the most important being in a parrot's life is the parrot himself!

This can help explain why it may not be easy to get your brand new ballpoint pen out from your macaw's beak. In that moment, the pen belongs to your bird. There is no sharing. That is until something more intriguing comes along, or that pen just becomes tiresome.

The author used positive reinforcement to train storks to sit calmly and await their food. Prior to this, the storks were aggressive—and dangerous—to keepers and each other during feeding time.

One training challenge I encountered while consulting at a zoo was aggressive behavior involving two storks. Storks are pretty formidable creatures. They can be quite large and have enormous beaks. These two storks would display aggressive behavior toward the keeper as the keeper entered the enclosure to clean. These two birds also showed a great deal of aggression when a tub containing their diet for the day (fish) was placed in the enclosure. One bird in particular seemed to be more forceful than the other and would deliberately chase the less confident stork away from the food bowl. There was concern one bird was simply not getting enough food. Two bowls did not seem to work as the stronger stork would simply aggress around both bowls. To address the aggression problems, we decided to train the birds to stand or station on two wooden discs placed at different sides of the enclosure. Our hope was that we could tell the birds to go to the discs before the keeper entered to avoid aggression with the keeper. The keeper could then toss food to each bird separately, thus avoiding aggression over the food. We were excited when after just a few weeks both birds learned to calmly station on their discs and await their food. We later slipped a scale on the discs and were able to weigh the birds quite easily as well. It is rewarding to change a potentially dangerous and stressful situation into a calm and positive interaction.

An interesting phenomenon we see in parrots is aggression around food bowls. This one is difficult to categorize because at times it straddles two different categories. In some cases, birds are extremely territorial and this territorial behavior seems to carry over into other areas as well. This may include areas outside of the cage, people and objects, such as food bowls. In these cases you will see birds behave aggressively if anyone comes near their food bowls. Even birds that are not displaying territorial aggression may also aggress when their food bowls are touched. In this case perhaps the classification falls into possession aggression.

Other examples of aggression that might result from the attempted removal of items includes aggression in regard to food, mates, and offspring. Food and access to a mate can be critical to a bird's survival in the wild. Of course, guarding offspring ensures survival of the species and the individual bird's lineage. It makes sense to a bird on an innate level to guard these resources. Attempts at removing these resources can lead to aggression, even if the companion owner knows these resources may be returned. In that moment the bird has no way of knowing this and responds in a manner that seems reasonable to a bird with a strong survival instinct. Instinctual drives that tell a bird to be aggressive can sometimes be challenging to address. However, they are not impossible to overcome. The pages ahead will examine strategies to deal with aggressive behavior in circumstances of possession aggression.

Excitement That Turns Into Aggression

Play behavior has been studied extensively in animals. It is said that play is a way for animals to practice skills required for survival. Play also stimulates the mind and body in ways that can be healthful and enriching. In parrots, play can help keep beaks from overgrowing, prevent muscle atrophy, stimulate arthritic joints, and more. Play is usually something animals engage in when their physical and psychological needs are met. In other words, it can signify that your bird is happy and healthy. Therefore seeing a bird playing is usually satisfying to the companion parrot owner. Participating with your parrot in the play activity can be even more rewarding — except when things get too rough. Just as with other animals, sometimes play behavior crosses the line of fun. In some cases, it is just ignorance on the part of the bird. For example, a young parrot may start exploring something with his mouth out of curiosity, like your finger, and then use a bit too much pressure. The bird has not learned this is not acceptable for you. In this situation, it is unlikely aggressive motivations are at work. It is more likely that curiosity and investigation became too intense for human flesh.

In another situation, a bird and companion parrot owner may be playing and the bird's excitement level rises and rises. Often the bird and the owner are vocalizing loudly and in high-pitched tones. It is in these moments a parrot may bite too hard in excitement. It is almost as if the bird is unable to contain himself from the overstimulation.

Another common scenario is the one in which the phone rings and the parrot in the household becomes charged up by the loud conversation. This can be quite exciting, especially if the bird is accustomed to a quiet situation. The bird may start to pin his eyes (the pupil becomes small in size), fluff up a bit, fan his tail feathers and

Some parrots will attempt to bite their owners when the food bowls are removed for cleaning and feeding. This is possession aggression. The parrot sees this as trying to protect his food resources from theft.

maybe join in the vocalizations. This is probably not the best time to have this bird sitting on your person. Perhaps this bird has responded to your heightened level of activity as you participate in the conversation. This, in turn, results in heightened levels of excitement in your bird, which again can lead to aggressive behaviors. Sometimes vacuum cleaners, running water, blow dryers, blenders, etc. can also trigger this same type of reaction. It would be interesting to observe and study how different species react when noise and activity levels in the environment vary. It certainly seems to be common that many parrots respond vigorously to increased auditory stimuli.

This is also similar to the situation in which the household is quiet all day, but then the entire family comes home. Lots of excitement ensues as kids release their pent-up energy, the kitchen bustles with activity as dinner is made, phones ring, and loud conversations travel through the house. The result is usually a very wound-up bird, responding to all the stimuli he has suddenly received. Again, this bird may be in state that is conducive to aggressive behaviors. Perhaps

When a parrot gets overexcited, he may suddenly lash out and bite. It seems that some birds cannot contain themselves from the overstimulation.

giving everyone time to settle down before handling the bird, would set the bird and the family up for a successful interaction.

Studies with rats have shown that arousal is frequently an outcome of aggressive behavior. Arousal in itself can be reinforcing and can increase the likelihood of further aggressive behavior. It is interesting to note that after a parrot exhibits aggressive behavior he typically continues to exhibit some aggressive body language. Some birds will strut, some will pin their eyes, some raise their crests, some vocalize. Most companion parrot owners learn quickly to give their bird a bit of distance after an aggressive display. These observations demonstrate that parrots are also certainly capable of having heightened levels of excitement as an outcome of aggression as well as a potential precursor.

Social Aggression

It is a curious study to watch parrots interacting with each other. Typically we are used to seeing new dog friends greet each other with enthusiasm and play for hours, although certainly not all dogs get along. Parrots in the home don't usually seem to be quite as enthusiastic about other birds unless, of course, they believe they have found the love of their lives. Then they seem to become stalkers that just won't leave the other bird alone. It is not uncommon to see birds that find another parrot to be the one and only companion they will tolerate. Birds that are raised together as a group and housed in a sufficient enclosure usually can get along as well for a while. Often as sexual maturity hits, birds pair off and become less tolerant of other individuals in their space.

At times, some species can be found in flock situations in the wild. When watching individuals interact in these groups, it is not uncommon to see minor displays of aggression as birds communicate what are acceptable and not acceptable behaviors amongst flock members. Rarely, if ever, do birds in the wild fight to the point of drawing blood. This has only been observed during serious battles over nest sites. The small signals birds give with their body language that indicate aggression are usually well recognized and respected by flock members. Parrots observe these signals and usually respond appropriately to avoid serious aggression. Humans on the other hand are often not quite as adept at reading and heeding these signals. It is a skill that can be acquired. After examining the different categories of aggression we will take a closer look at how to read and interpret aggressive body language.

Birds, like other animals, can sometimes show aggression when confinement forces them to share a space with other individuals. Studies on primates have shown that when new members are introduced to an established group significant increases in aggressive behavior occur. The aggression is all targeted toward the new members of the group. A strategy that is often used in the zoo community to see how animals that have never met might get along is to place the animals in separate enclosures that are close to one another and allow the animals to see each other without physical contact. The term often used to describe this procedure is *howdy*. The two animals can then be observed to see how they react towards each other. If they seem to be nonaggressive, the two enclosures can be moved closer and eventually the animals are placed in the same enclosure. Howdying two animals is

Parrots can be horribly aggressive to other parrots at times. These cockatiels have had their feather follicles permanently damaged by other cockatiels, and it is unlikely that their feathers will grow back.

a nice way to help them safely get to know each other.

Some birds simply do not adjust to new birds or sharing an enclosure. It is not uncommon to hear about aggressive behavior occurring when two cockatoos are paired for breeding. Sometimes even the largest cage is not enough to reduce the aggression. Social structure of parrot species can vary dramatically and can be very complex. Certainly we have a lot to learn about this area. In the meantime, the best strategy is to observe your bird's behavior around other birds. If your bird is not comfortable with other birds, it may be best to respect your bird's wishes and keep strange birds at a distance.

Most hand-raised parrots seem to view a human as just another parrot. Perhaps that is why a little 300-gram parrot can strut around with such confidence around a 150-pound human—and sometimes send a 150-pound person running for cover. Getting along with another bird may not be that important for you and your bird. However, getting along with other people may be important. While some birds may not be inclined to interact with many people on their own, it is possible to

Height and Dominance

Height dominance is a fairly new concept that has been introduced into the companion parrot culture. The idea is that if a parrot is perched higher than the head of another individual (bird or human), the parrot perceives himself as having a dominant role in the relationship. There are a few factors at work that may have lead to this theory. One factor is that humans can relate to dominance and respect for a dominant or authoritative figure. Humans also many times are raised with the notion that humans are dominant to animals and need to control animals. Finally, it is not uncommon for a parrot to appear to be more confident and comfortable when perched high as opposed to sitting on the ground. This ties into a parrot's strategy for survival. Sitting high allows a bird a good opportunity to keep an eye out for predators and also allows a bird to attain lift easily for flight. Being low on the ground makes a bird an easy target. Either by instinct or learning

In nature, parrots feel most safe and secure when they are on high perches. Being up high is positively reinforcing to a parrot, and he may react aggressively if a keeper tries to make him come down.

parrots have discovered being elevated is good survival strategy. A confident and comfortable elevated bird may be less likely to obey a command to come down. But then again, why should the bird want to come down? His perception is that being higher is safer. This may lead to the interpretation that the bird's disobedience is about him feeling dominant or in control of the companion parrot owner.

If one looks at the behavior from a training perspective, there are many positive reasons for the bird to want to remain perched high and less value in sitting low. From the birds perspective it probably has very little to do with dominance. It is simply more positively reinforcing to remain high than to move lower. Rather than trying to force the bird to obey and return to the companion parrot owner, focus on training the bird to return for positive reinforcement.

In addition to an analysis of the theories, my personal experience of free-flying birds in shows for 15 years has also taught me that the mechanisms at work are simple reinforcement values. It is not uncommon for parrots to occasionally wander off course in a show and end up sitting high in a tree. Climbing a tree to retrieve a bird usually is not an option. Therefore, training birds to fly to trainers for positive reinforcement is the reasonable choice. Can you imagine trying to command a parrot to fly from a 50 ft tree? Trying to use force and dominance to retrieve a free-flighted bird is nearly impossible. And if dominance or attempted force is used, the bird will have learned to stay farther away in the future. A bird can easily learn to return to the hand for positive reinforcement. It works over and over again. One of the incredible benefits of working with animals that have the choice to go wherever they want is that trainers must learn the art of applying good training strategies based on positive reinforcement in order to obtain behavior. The animal can leave if they do not like any part of the experience. The next time your bird sits on the curtain rod and doesn't want to leave, pull out the peanuts and show your bird that being with you is better than the curtain rod!

teach a bird to accept other people for positive reinforcement. Young birds are often very receptive to new things. A companion parrot owner can take advantage of that window of opportunity to expose a young bird to many people while associating positive consequences for the bird for interacting with new individuals. As this bird matures, he or she is more likely to be receptive to being handled by strangers or other members of the household as long as positive reinforcement is maintained for this behavior.

Social aggression is quite complex and includes a wide range of scenarios. Some situations are more challenging to address than others. Sometimes the best choice is to reconsider what level of social behavior is required for you and your bird to be happy.

Learned by Practice Aggression

One of the most common ways aggression is developed and perpetuated is by learning. This concept can sometimes be a hard one for the companion parrot owner to grasp. Perhaps it is because it means we may have played a part in creating the aggressive behavior. The

If you need to introduce two parrots, it is useful to howdy them before putting them together. This involves keeping the birds separated but near each other for a few days and observing how they react.

good news is once a companion parrot owner recognizes her role in the process she can move toward solutions to learned aggression. Let's look at some typical scenarios in which a parrot learns to be aggressive.

Many companion parrot owners have been told that their bird *must* obey the step up command. This information has lead many a brave soul to thrust their hand into a cage and promptly get bit. The bite may have caused a few people to withdraw their hand. In that moment, the parrot just learned, "If I bite the hand when it comes at me, it will go away." What is usually observed next time is that the bird immediately shows body language that he intends to bite when he sees a hand coming. How a bird reacts when he sees a hand can tell you a lot about his history with hands and forced interactions.

I have trained vultures to fly from towers, monkeys to sit on scales, crows to retrieve objects, skunks to dig on cue, and owls to swoop over people's heads. One of the most challenging training situations I encountered was training a collection of birds in a parrot sanctuary to step up on the hand for positive reinforcement. I had trained many birds for free-flight bird programs prior to this. I had not worked with so many previously owned pets at the same time. (Birds for shows usually are acquired through breeding programs and their training can begin when the birds are quite young and very open to new things. Usually they have not had a lot of negative history with other people.) What I found so remarkable was just how many of these second-hand birds demonstrated a learned aggressive behavior toward hands. I typically teach a bird to step up on my hand for positive reinforcement by placing my hand on a perch outside of the cage and allowing the bird to choose to walk across it to receive a treat. I never come at the bird with my hand while the bird is learning the behavior. Almost all of these birds would make an effort to bite the hand aggressively as they approached it. Usually, a fearful bird will go away from what he fears when given the opportunity. These birds had the freedom to go where they pleased; however, these birds chose to try to bite. This lead me to believe that it was likely in their past experiences they did not have the freedom to go where they pleased and were forced to cope with hands in unpleasant interactions. I had to use my ability to read bird behavior very carefully to avoid some nasty bites. It was a long and sometimes

One of the most common ways aggression is developed and perpetuated is by learning. If a parrot learns that biting gets rid of an unwanted stimulus (like a hand), he has learned that biting will get him what he wants.

nerve-wracking process, but eventually every bird did learn to step up on the hand without trying to bite for positive reinforcement. What was most astonishing to me is the number of birds that demonstrated this learned aggression. It causes me to think there is a great need to educate bird owners and owners-to-be so that both the birds and the people can achieve the best relationship possible without fear, aversives, punishment, or aggression.

Another example of learned aggression occurs when a parrot does not want to go back into the cage. Some parrots have a wonderful relationship with their companion parrot owners. This becomes a challenge when it is time to go back in the cage. The parrot would prefer to be out. Here is what often transpires: As the companion parrot owner approaches the cage with the parrot on the hand, the parrot leans down and chomps the owner's hand. The owner may then bring the bird away from the cage to get him to stop biting. This just reinforced the biting. The next time the owner goes to put the bird back in the cage, it is very likely the bird will repeat the aggressive behavior. This doesn't mean in the future the owner should take the bite and forge ahead and put the bird in the cage. Instead we will explore positive ways to get the bird back in the cage without biting.

How Did Paco the Amazon Parrot Get to Be 100 Years Old?

On occasion, one hears about a remarkable bird in a family that reached 100 years old or more. Usually it has been passed on from one family member to another family member. Accurate records on individual birds that date back 100 years are pretty difficult to find, but records from zoos and other facilities have shown that most parrots do not live quite that long on average. One exception was a cockatoo at the London Zoo that died at the age of at least 80 years old. There have also been claims that a parrot once owned by Winston Churchill is currently 104 years old. This claim has been contested and so far still remains an uncertainty. But these long-lived individuals are rare and without accurate documentation difficult to prove. We have learned a great deal in recent years about the best health care practices for captive parrots. It is possible current trends in animal care and future discoveries will lead to longer life spans. In the case of Paco the 100-year-old Amazon, it is most likely the original Paco died at a reasonable age for an Amazon parrot and was replaced by another bird that inherited the name Paco. If that happened often enough, it would be easy to see how Paco obtained legendary status as the immortal Amazon parrot!

Amazon parrots can be long-lived animals, sometimes reaching over 50 years old. Very few will reach 100 years, although the myth of the 100-year-old parrot persists in popular culture.

Some situations to avoid seem obvious. Once an aggression interaction has started, sometimes it is difficult to remain clear-headed in thought and choose the appropriate course of action. One typical scenario is when the bird has just bitten or is in the middle of an aggressive act. Some well-meaning individuals will offer a treat, such as a peanut, to distract the bird and to interrupt the bird's biting or aggressive behavior. Unfortunately, as expected, this reinforces the aggressive behavior and teaches the bird aggressive acts can result in a treat. Once again a parrot has learned to be aggressive.

In addition to things companion parrot owners do to reinforce aggression, birds can also learn to be aggressive by watching other birds. Parrots are famous for their ability to mimic sounds, but they also imitate body postures and will also model behavior of other parrots. Have you ever seen a flock of parrots disperse immediately after one parrot flies away in fear? Again, sometimes it is a good survival strategy for a parrot to pay attention to what his neighbor is doing. Your neighbor might be able to alert you to danger or when it is safe to eat or bathe. Imitating behavior is an observable phenomenon in parrots. Be aware that if one parrot is demonstrating aggressive behaviors, it is possible another parrot in the household can learn by observing this behavior.

There are countless examples in which aggressive behavior gets reinforced. Usually it is not our intention to reinforce these unpleasant behaviors. Understanding how aggression works and how it is learned can help prevent future events of learned aggression.

Frustration Aggression

Animal training can really be a fascinating profession. If done well, a trained behavior looks smooth and effortless. This appearance of ease may underestimate the complexities of using operant conditioning principles effectively. Not suprisingly, poor training decisions can create aggressive behavior. You may be asking yourself, "What has this got to do with me and my bird? I am not a trainer." On the contrary, every bird owner is a trainer. You may be a seasoned veteran who has taught your bird a number of behaviors, or you may just love to spend quality time with your bird. Either way, your bird is learning from his interactions with you. And training is just a formalized method of teaching.

This formalized method is really a set of tools that gives a language that both the people and the animals can understand. It is a form of communication. As we all know, communication can break down. Sometimes people fail to read, interpret, and respect the body language of animals. And sometimes it takes time for an animal to decipher what it is we want. These communication errors can actually result in aggressive behavior.

I recall watching a dolphin training session during a consultation. One dolphin had no interest in eating fish. She was pregnant and required by management to receive a certain amount of food each day to facilitate her pregnancy. The dolphins typically received their food during a training session. Each animal was positioned with a trainer to prevent food competition and to engage in some training. The trainer would ask the particular dolphin to perform a behavior. She would comply, but usually she would also slap the side of the pool with her tail flukes aggressively as well. When she returned she would refuse food if offered and try to bite at the trainers hand. The trainer would repeatedly ask for the behavior, and she would comply along with the aggressive response.

Frustration can make both birds and people aggressive. Asking your bird to perform a behavior that is too challenging for him can lead to frustration aggression.

In this case, it appeared several things were occurring that influenced her aggression. One problem was that the dolphin was not motivated to participate in the session at that moment in time. Food, attention, toys—none of these things were reinforcing to the animal at that moment. Another problem was the repeated request for the behavior. In this case, pushing for more behavior could have contributed to frustration and further influenced the aggression. Finally, the dolphin was given many opportunities to practice these aggressive displays, and practice makes perfect. Later we will discuss the liabilities in allowing an animal to rehearse aggressive behavior. All these factors lead to a challenging situation. In this scenario, probably the best choice would have been to walk away and consider having a session later when the animal was more receptive.

This same scenario can apply to your bird at home. Trying to interact with a bird that is not motivated or showing aggressive behavior could also result in an unsuccessful encounter. There are other practices that may cause your bird to be frustrated and show aggression as well. For example, it is possible for an animal to learn to expect a steady stream of reinforcement. This sometimes happens when we get very excited about offering treats to a bird. A drawback can be that a

Studies in sheep have proven that bad training can cause frustration aggression. Breaking a behavior down into simpler steps can help avoid frustration.

bird learns not to be patient and may aggress while frustration builds waiting for the next treat.

Another aggression situation can occur when we ask a bird to do more than they are currently capable of doing. A behavior that is too physically challenging can cause frustration. In addition, any animal that is feeling sick or tired may also be at risk for displaying aggressive behaviors.

Another common scenario is unclear communication. When we teach an animal a new behavior, we usually break the behavior down into small steps or parts and reward success after each step. However, sometimes we can make those steps too big. The animal is unsure of what we want. If we continue to push the animal into trying to figure it out, the end result can be aggression. It is much better to take that big step and break it down into smaller steps to help the bird understand and avoid confusion that can lead to frustration and possible aggression.

Some people are familiar with the concept of using a clicker to train a bird. The clicker is just a sound or signal that lets the bird know it has done something correct and reinforcement is to follow. Another term for the clicker is "bridging stimulus" or "bridge" for short. It is called a bridge because it bridges the gap in time between when the behavior was performed correctly and when the reinforcement will be received. The bridge can be any signal the trainer chooses (a clicker, a whistle, a light, a touch, etc.). The most important thing about the bridge is how you use it. It is very important that the bridge happens right at the moment the trainer sees the behavior he or she wants. But it has also been shown that what happens after the bridge is important as well.

Behavior analysis students at the University of North Texas in Denton conducted a study as to what happens when the delivery of the reinforcement after the bridge is delayed. This was done with a sheep. The sheep was trained to touch a red spot on the ground with her nose. When she did this, the bridge would sound and reinforcement was delivered immediately. Over time the students would wait longer and longer to give the reinforcement after the bridge. At first the animal would offer different behaviors in an effort to receive the reinforcement. The sheep also began to display her frustration by pawing at the ground; fortunately this frustration did not develop into serious aggression. (A sheep can be pretty strong!) Eventually the sheep gave up and stopped participating. In this study, it was clear this animal achieved a level of frustration caused by the actions of the trainer.

Other training strategies can also lead to aggression. There is a strategy called "extinguishing the behavior" or "taking a behavior to extinction." In this strategy, the idea is to reduce or eliminate a behavior by not reinforcing it. This can be a very effective tool when used properly. This technique can also create a level of frustration in an animal if it is not used in conjunction with other training strategies. That is why it is often paired with positive reinforcement of another acceptable behavior, steps towards that behavior, or any behavior other than the one that is desired to be extinguished. This may seem like a complex idea, but in reality it is a concept we described earlier—ignore bad behavior and reward good.

Frustration usually builds over time. Fortunately this is helpful to the companion parrot owner because it means there is an opportunity to observe behavior that indicates frustration before aggression occurs. Learn to recognize those signals early to avoid frustration aggression. These signals can include non-performance of the cued behavior, a tendency to be easily distracted, lack of interest in positive reinforcement when offered, slow response to cues, and more. These signals can also sometimes indicate poor training strategy has been applied. Therefore, it important to look at the overall situation when deciding how to proceed.

Personal Aggression

Have you ever had an animal dislike you for no apparent reason? You cannot think of anything you could have possibly done that would have caused you to be the object of aggression, yet still you seem to be singled out as a target for aggressive behavior by that animal. Unfortunately, I experienced this situation with a little tiny monkey. Her name was Sherry and she was a saki monkey. While consulting at a zoo, I often found myself walking by this little monkey's exhibit. She lived in a giant tree on an island. Whenever I walked by she would grimace, emphatically bounce the tree limbs, and look ready to leap off the tree if I would only get a little closer. It is possible she behaved this way because every day I walked by her exhibit; every day she displayed

If a parrot dislikes a specific person for no known reason, he is exhibiting personal aggression. Sometimes a slight change in appearance and some positive reinforcement can correct this problem.

at me; every day I went away after she displayed; and then came back again the very next day! How rewarding for her that I would leave after her displays and how very frustrating for her that I would return! I later also learned she had a history of displaying aggressively at women who looked like me. It is possible that somewhere in her past she had a very negative experience with someone who looked like me, but certainly my walking route was not helping the situation. My opportunity to modify the situation came when she was transferred to another holding area after she had given birth. I pushed my hair up under a hat to alter my appearance and came bearing gifts — walnuts and marshmallows, that is. Sherry and I began a new relationship that day. She quickly learned to touch a target with her hand, and gently accepted food from me. Over time, I gradually let my hair out from under the hat without incident. So despite our rocky beginnings, we worked out our differences.

Personal aggression sometimes has no obvious explanation. Sometimes it does. For example, we often see animals that are nervous

One study shows that the first experience an animal has with a person has a lasting impact on how that animal reacts to that person in the future.

of the veterinarian. Although the veterinarian is doing something to help, the process is not always comfortable for the animals. It is easy for an animal to then associate negative experiences with the veterinarian and show fear and or aggressive behaviors when the veterinarian is nearby. I will never forget being charged by a lion when I happened to walk by the enclosure with the staff veterinarian at an exotic cat sanctuary. The veterinarian was responsible for darting cats when necessary. The power of a large cat is never to be underestimated.

It can be very challenging to overcome personal aggression, but not impossible. One study shows the first experience an animal has with an object or person has tremendous impact. If that first experience is perceived as positive by the animal, that positive association can help override future negative interactions. If that first experience is negative, it will be harder to overcome the negative association and change it to positive. This emphasizes how important it is to try to set your bird up for positive experiences with new people, places and things, especially when it is the first encounter.

Chapter 5

Reading Bird Body Language

Aparrot has a distinctive language. We see that language every day—it is their body language. Birds hold their feathers, their eyes, their limbs, in certain postures that indicate certain states of mind. It is practically unconscious for birds. Usually a bird does not appear to necessarily be thinking about expressing himself; he just does it. What is also interesting is that it appears that parrots expect us to understand what they are saying with their body language. And many times we do understand. Isn't it fascinating that despite our biological differences, humans can often learn to decipher what our companion animals want?

In the animal training world this is described as the ability to read and interpret an animal's body language. The best animal trainers are ones that are outstanding at reading body language and adjusting what they are doing to make the animal as comfortable as he can be. Excellent trainers do whatever they can to avoid fear and aggression and to help create a pleasant environment for an animal. These adjustments can be very, very subtle, just as the body language of the animal can be subtle.

Remember in the discussion on height dominance, it was mentioned that oftentimes birds prefer to be elevated because it helps them to feel safe and ready for take off. I often employed this method when carrying a hawk on my gloved hand. Hawks are certainly different from parrots, but they also display body language to indicate their level of comfort. Usually a trainer carries a hawk perched on a glove on his or her left hand. After years of experience, trainers are usually quite sensitive to the feel of the bird on the glove. It is possible to feel if a bird is nervous just by the simple movements he may make. Often a hawk that is nervous will bounce or spring up a little as if he is getting ready to take off into flight and/or put his wings out to the side. If I noted this feeling I would often consider a few options. One option was to stop going where I was going and let the bird look around for a moment and desensitize to the environment. Another action I might take was to raise the bird up a little in the air. Often just this little lift helped the bird relax. All of this may seem like a lot of shifting and adjusting to accommodate birds. However, after a period of time, the birds learned to feel quite confident that I would take action to ensure their comfort. This in turn benefited the relationship I had with the birds.

Good parrot owners will learn to read and be responsive to their bird's body language. The elevated crest of this palm cockatoo signals that he is very excited—perhaps by the camera lens.

This type of sensitivity works wonders when applied to parrots as well. In my experience with free-flight bird shows, birds showed better response to trainers who showed better sensitivity to bird behavior. Sometimes during shows, birds would fly to locations for which they were not intended. The birds were well trained to fly to a trainer's hand. If by chance a bird was sitting in a nearby tree, different trainers may take turns calling the bird to the hand. An interesting pattern emerged. Typically birds responded more rapidly to the trainers that demonstrated the most sensitivity to bird behavior. The birds did not necessarily respond to the person with whom they may have had the most history, rather they responded to the person with whom they had the *best* history.

The importance of sensitivity to bird behavior cannot be underestimated. Becoming proficient at reading and responding to bird body language can change a companion parrot's owner's relationship with his or her bird dramatically. Consider trying to interact with a companion parrot that is terrified to come out of a cage. I once worked with an umbrella cockatoo at a parrot sanctuary that was quite frightened to leave his cage. His name was Casper. Casper greatly enjoyed attention and the opportunity to interact with people but only within the cage or through the bars. Any attempt to pass the bird through the door of the cage would cause Casper to leap back into the cage. In my opinion, forcing him thorough the doorway would have been so traumatic that it had the potential to destroy any trust this bird had in humans. It also had the potential to create an aggressive response motivated by fear. Because of this, I decided to train Casper to leave the cage for positive reinforcement. I anticipated it would be a relatively long process and it was. I began by opening the door of the cage and then sitting on the floor in front of the cage. Casper would climb down to the bottom of the cage for attention and his favorite treats (peanuts and pine nuts). Initially, I just fed him and offered attention for being in the area. I then focused on teaching him to step up on the hand for a food treat right at the edge of the door. It took a few weeks of daily 20-minute training sessions for Casper to learn to step up on the hand in this location. I imagine his progress may have been slow in part due to the fact that in the past stepping up on the hand had been followed up with

This sensitive owner has picked up on her macaw's fear of his travel cage. By going slowly and offering him some rewards, she should be able to relax her bird and turn this into a positive interaction.

a forced attempt to get Casper out of the cage. This, of course, was an extremely negative experience for Casper, and one he did not wish to repeat. Once he did learn to step up for positive reinforcement in the form of food, I focused on gradually moving him away from the cage. The moment Casper showed any fear I allowed him to return to the cage. It took several weeks more for Casper to finally learn to be confident enough to be several feet outside of this cage. Once he was becoming more comfortable being outside of the cage, I also incorporated sessions in which Casper could sit on my lap and receive lots of head scratches and all over attention. If anything frightened him, he was always offered the opportunity to return to his cage. This breakthrough for Casper also allowed me to train him to step onto a scale and enter a kennel voluntarily. It was a long road of very small approximations and sensitivity to Casper's comfort, but the payoff was tremendous. It was extremely rewarding for me as a trainer to see an animal learn to overcome such fears. It opened the door for a richer life for a bird that desperately wanted to interact but was limited by his fears.

Sensitivity to Casper's body language was critical to the success of his training. Any small signal that indicated fear needed to be respected and adjustments needed to be made to make sure Casper was as comfortable as possible. This strategy is important any time interactions with a companion parrot are occurring.

Developing Sensitivity to Companion Parrot Behavior

For some people it can be challenging to try to avoid causing fear and aggressive responses in their companion parrots. Often people are focused on the end result of the task they desire and not on the process. In other words, they just want the bird to do whatever it is they are asking, such as step up, return to the cage, or get in the kennel. What I hope to emphasize here is that taking time to focus on making the process as positive as possible for your companion parrot may take longer, but it is worth it, as the desired result can be attained without experiencing aggressive behavior from the companion parrot. Once the bird has gone through a pleasant process to learn the desired behavior a companion

When interacting with your bird in a new situation, ask yourself, "What is he thinking?" Doing this will sensitize you to your bird's level of comfort.

parrot owner will have gained two important things: a bird that looks forward to doing the desired task (and will do it quite readily), and an amazing relationship based on trust with his or her bird.

The easiest way for a companion parrot owner to begin the journey to heightened sensitivity to bird behavior is to slow down when interacting with a companion parrot. Slow down and allow for time to read and interpret the bird's body language. A companion parrot owner can then ask himself or herself, "What is the bird thinking?" It is important to be really honest when asking this question. If a favorite bird is showing aggressive behavior, it may hurt that individual's feelings, but the truth is the bird is showing aggression. If the companion parrot owner wants a better relationship with that bird, it is in the best interest of the companion parrot owner to recognize and accept the bird is showing aggression. The companion parrot owner can then respond in a way to improve that situation.

Another helpful strategy is to recognize that quite probably, birds are reading and reacting to our body language far more than we are reading and reacting to theirs. By recognizing this, we can also learn to be more aware of our own actions and the effects they can have on bird behavior.

Every interaction with your bird is a learning experience for both of you, and every interaction affects that relationship.

When a companion parrot owner intends on interacting with a bird, even in the most routine ways (weighing, picking up, etc.), sensitivity can be improved by focusing attention on the task at hand. Focus on reading the bird's behavior and adjusting companion parrot owner behavior. Focus on being sensitive. It is important for the companion parrot owner to never forget when he or she has a bird on his or her hand. It is easy to get distracted by conversation, activity, etc. Staying in touch with the bird can make even this seemingly basic interaction more successful.

Also important to remember is the concept that every interaction counts. Every interaction is a learning experience for that bird (and the companion parrot owner). Every interaction can affect the relationship between the bird and the companion parrot owner. A better quality interaction (brought about because the companion parrot owner is focused) can lead to a better relationship and better odds of good behavior from the bird. It is much like tunnel vision, as the companion parrot owner enters into the interaction. The companion parrot owner's world becomes small as he or she focuses on the interaction.

Even if the companion parrot owner is not intentionally interacting with a bird, if the bird is aware of the companion parrot owner's presence, he or she is affecting his or her relationship with that bird. Territorial behaviors can start way before companion parrot owners get close to the bird. Ignoring these behaviors can have serious repercussions.

It is also important to be aware of environmental distractions. A new person walking into the room may trigger aggression; a dog jumping up may frighten an unsuspecting bird; a higher perch nearby may be an appealing place for a bird to perch even though the companion parrot owner would like the bird to stay on his or her hand. In these situations, companion parrot owners must be aware of the surroundings and adjust accordingly. Perhaps the companion parrot owner blocks the bird's view of the perch or the dog. The companion parrot owner could also positively reinforce the bird for staying on the hand when they may not normally do so. Birds need not be startled or nervous of environmental factors if an observant companion parrot owner anticipates what might scare his or her parrot. Again, it is the companion parrot owner's responsibility to notice this behavior and expect the need to adjust it.

With birds, small things count a lot. A companion parrot owner's small movements can be big to the bird. In addition, the bird's small movements, to a sensitive companion parrot owner, are also big. Birds are incredibly observant. It is important for companion parrot owners to challenge themselves to be as perceptive about how *their* behavior is affecting the bird's behavior. Companion parrot owners can look for small changes in bird body language to cue to themselves that something is going on which is affecting the bird's behavior. Certainly many companion parrot owners have had a bird stop playing or preening and look at something with a cocked head and perhaps even growl a bit. The companion parrot owner looks to see what the bird sees and there is a little tiny speck of a spider crawling on the ceiling. But companion parrot owners also need to focus on even smaller behavior changes. A simple quick look with the eyes to one side may mean the bird is looking for an escape path and is ready to take off.

Another way to help increase sensitivity is to treat every interaction as if it was the first time it has happened. Just because in the past a bird has always stepped up onto a companion parrot owner's hand, it does not necessarily mean it is going to step up today. Animals are not robots. It is unfair of us to assume every interaction will be the same. Again, it is a more sensitive companion parrot owner that takes the time to read every situation before proceeding. And again, in the long term, it can effect the companion parrot owner/bird relationship and increase the bird's response to that individual.

Understanding the theory behind the suggestions to help develop sensitivity to bird behavior is important. However, it can be difficult to conceptualize. The following is a list of examples in which a companion parrot owner can apply sensitivity to bird behavior and potentially see results in the form of a better bird/companion parrot owner relationship and better behavior.

- Picking up a bird: the bird willingly steps onto the companion parrot owner's hand for positive reinforcement and little or no negative reinforcement.
- Moving birds in kennels or cages is as smooth and steady as it can possibly be.

- Birds are not "accidentally" frightened by strange objects. Companion parrot owners are careful when bringing/moving items near birds that might scare or startle their birds. Companion parrot owners allow birds time to desensitize to a new environment, new person, object etc., rather than expect acceptance or tolerance in a new situation right away.
- Birds are not forced off the hand if they won't get on a perch. Companion parrot owners focus on patiently training the behavior with positive reinforcement.
- Companion parrot owners do not drop a bird or wiggle him while on the hand to get him to put his wings out.

Obviously parrots' body language covers a huge range of categories. The more a companion parrot owner can observe and understand the better. The two most important types of body language to look for are fear and aggression. Fear is included in this section because a bird that is afraid may resort to aggression. I am sure many companion parrot owners have heard of the fight-or-flight response. This describes what typically happens in the first stage of stress, also known as the alarm reaction stage. The goal for a sensitive companion parrot owner is to never create the type of stress that would cause a bird to want to fight or fly away.

How do you know what to look for to avoid fear and aggression? In the following section we will examine the specific body postures that indicate an aggressive state and a fearful state. There are over 300 species of parrots. Therefore the focus will be on some broad categories. There will be overlaps of behavioral displays for different groups of bird species, but unique characteristics of types of parrot will also be described.

I learned how challenging it is to look for specific characteristics of behavior when I was teaching a workshop on training and behavior to zoo professionals. I explained that a bird the group was training appeared to be nervous. One of the assistants asked, "How do you know?" That was a very important question. Instead of listening to gut instinct to ascertain what mental state a bird might be experiencing, it forced me to really look objectively at the body posture of the animal. It also forced me to make note of specific details that I was observing that would lead me to believe this animal was feeling nervous. Additionally, I had to find words to describe what I was seeing, so that the students could also learn to look for the same specific postures when working with a bird.

This question taught me to be more observant and more detailed in my observation of bird behavior. I think it is a great exercise for every companion parrot owner to try with their bird at home or any other bird they can observe. First, observe a bird and try to decide what the mental state of the bird is at the time. Is he comfortable, nervous, tired, aggressive, anxious, etc.? Then ask yourself, "How do I know? What specific body language do I see that tells me this is what a bird is thinking or feeling?" You may even want to write down what you observe or take pictures or video. Sometimes it is easier to study video or photos, since you have the opportunity to review them over and over again. In addition you will have a wonderful collection of information on your bird in the event someone else must care for your bird in the future.

One important thing to note about parrot behavior is that it can be extremely subtle. We will discuss some general and obvious

One of the first signs of aggression in many parrot species (illustrated here by a blue and gold macaw [left] and a peach-faced lovebird) is the raising of feathers on the nape. As the aggression intensifies, more feathers on the neck and some on the back of the head will rise. When the bird reaches a high level of aggression, the feathers on shoulders and upper back will rise.

characteristics of displays of fear and aggression. We are also going to focus on the smallest signals as well. This is because when a companion parrot owner is interacting with his or her bird, the goal is to notice the signs of fear and aggression as early as possible. This allows the companion parrot owner to take action to address the problems well before anyone gets hurt. Remember, parrots in the wild are great at observing and respecting the small signals they give each other that indicate fear and aggression. Humans can develop this ability to notice these small signals as well.

Now let's look at the specific characteristics of aggressive body language in parrots.

What Does Aggression Look Like?
Feather Position

Often one of the first subtle signs of aggression is a change in feather position. The feathers to notice, in particular, are the feathers at the nape of the neck. In the early stage of aggression, usually all the feathers

Different species of parrots can have different body language, and a wise owner learns to recognize the body language of her bird. The raised head crest of a Leadbetter's cockatoo indicates fear or concern.

One of the most obvious indicators of aggression in parrots is eye pinning. This is the name given to the drastic reduction in the size of the pupil seen in parrots exhibiting aggressive behavior.

of the body are flat against the body except the feathers at the nape of the neck. These feathers will be the first to rise or fluff slightly. As aggression builds, more feathers on the sides of the neck may rise. Also, feathers on the head may rise as well. But it is important to note that usually not all the feathers on the head will rise. A significant distinction with aggression is that typically the feathers at the very front of the head, just above the beak do not rise much or at all. A relaxed bird will often have these front feathers raised forward. In aggressive birds this usually occurs to a much lesser degree.

As aggression increases, the number of feathers that are raised increases. But again, the feathers in question are those only in specific areas of the body. The next set of feathers that rise are those that span the shoulders and scapular part of the wing and back. When a bird has this many feathers raised, the bird has reached a very high level of aggression and is likely to bite.

Cockatoos, of course, indicate quite a bit about their state of mind by the movement of their very elaborate crest feathers. But they also tend to keep the very front feathers low in the early stage of aggression.

As aggression and or excitement builds, the crest feathers may rise.

In addition to raising feathers on the head neck and shoulders, some species of parrots will fan out tail feathers as an aggressive response. This can also happen when a state of excitement is achieved, which sometimes makes aggression hard to distinguish from excitement. However, looking at all the physical factors can better help a companion parrot owner ascertain the state of mind of the bird. This tail fanning is especially prominent in Amazon parrots, but can also be seen in macaws and cockatoos as well.

Eyes

The eyes of a parrot can communicate a great deal. The first thing to consider when looking at the eyes of a parrot is where the parrot's eyes are focused. Usually parrots look at what is first and foremost in their minds. If a bird has concern about a person's hand, the bird will usually look at the hand. Just like people, a parrot's eye may become wider when something has caused him to be on alert.

The most obvious indicator of potential aggression in parrot species is eye pinning. This is the name given for a parrot's fascinating ability to reduce the size of its pupil to a small pinpoint. Eye pinning allows much more of the iris to be seen. In the early stages of aggression, a companion parrot owner may notice only a small reduction in pupil size. As aggression builds, the pupil may decrease even more in size or may seem to vibrate. Some birds will alternate between a large pupil and a small pupil, creating what appears to be a flashing effect. A bird that is irritated enough to be flashing his pupils is in a heightened state of aggression.

Eye pinning is easier to see on species of parrots with light irises such as mature Amazon parrots, macaws, and African greys. Species with dark irises also perform this behavior. Looking close enough at the eyes of an aggressive sulphur-crested cockatoo will demonstrate this to be true—if you dare to get that close!

Mouth

The beak is a parrot's ultimate tool of defense if he cannot escape a perceived threat. Therefore, it is not uncommon to see some body

Holding the mouth open, grinding the beak, and moving the tongue around are all signs of potential aggression. Usually the parrot will orient the beak toward what he views as the target for the aggression.

language involving the beak that indicates aggression. Usually the parrot will orient the beak towards what he may view as his potential target. Sometimes the mouth will open slightly. Some birds will grind the tips of the upper and lower part of the beak together. Some will grind with what appears to be excessive force. In addition, some birds will move their tongues around a bit as if investigating something in the front part of their beaks. It almost has the appearance of preparing the mouth to bite.

Vocalizations

As a bird enters an aggressive state, it is not uncommon to hear some type of vocalization. Cockatoos may hiss. Many parrots will respond with a quick scream in response to something painful, such as companion parrot owner touching a blood feather, before aggressing. Some species also exhibit a sound that is best described as growling. This can be heard in large macaws and Amazon parrots especially. Usually, large-scale vocalization is not heard in connection with aggression in the home, unless fear is involved. This may happen if a bird was captured and restrained against his will.

Breathing

It may seem odd to consider breathing as a behavior to observe when looking for aggression, but we do sometimes see changes in breathing patterns when parrots approach aggressive states. Typically the breathing becomes more pronounced or agitated. A bird's breathing may appear to be more noticeable and audible.

Head Position

Initially a bird may draw his head back slightly in response to a stimulus he does not like. If the stimulus continues to move towards the bird, like an unwanted hand for example, often the bird's head drops immediately. Basically, the bird gets his head down closer to the object he may intend to bite. Birds will also swipe or lunge at an unwanted intrusion of a hand or other object. Usually other signals such as feathers and eyes indicate aggression before a bird resorts to lunging.

Wing Position

In the early stages of aggression, a parrot's wings may be flat against his sides. As aggression escalates, parrots may hold the wings out away from the body just slightly. This is often seen in conjunction with

Holding the wings out from the sides of the body indicates a heightened state of aggression. This hyacinth macaw is also holding open his beak and lunging—very obvious aggressive behaviors.

Macaws and some other parrot species that have bare facial areas exhibit flushing of this bare skin when experiencing aggressive states.

feathers on the shoulders and scapular part of the back fluffing up. Again, this is an advanced stage of aggression. The signals could have been observed and respected before this type of aggressive behavior occurs.

Facial Flushing

An interesting phenomenon that occurs in some parrots is facial flushing. Macaws have featherless patches of skin around the face. When experiencing aggressive states, the bare patch of skin on the face can become quite red. This is especially prominent in territorial macaws. This facial flushing can also been seen in palm cockatoos.

Movements

There is a wide variety of movements parrots can make that indicate aggression. Usually these occur in conjunction with the behaviors described above. One common movement a companion parrot owner might see before being bitten is displaced aggression.

Many times parrots will bite or lunge at something else when experiencing an aggressive state. We explored earlier how redirected aggression can occur, but it can be an excellent indicator of even more aggression to follow. Parrots will sometimes redirect aggression on toys, cage bars, and even themselves. My blue-fronted Amazon parrot will bite his own leg if the vacuum cleaner comes to close to his cage. Some parrots will viciously crumble their pellets. These can be important warning signs to the companion parrot owner to cease and desist in order to avoid more serious consequences.

Strutting seems to be another very obvious indicator of potential aggression. Usually this is seen in association with eye pining and tail fanning. A cockatoo may also have his crest raised and jump or bounce as he expresses his state of mind. I like to describe this as the "pumped up" bird. A bird in this state is extremely stimulated and has the potential to do some serious damage.

When looking for aggressive behavior, it is usually a combination of the characteristics described above that is observed. Parrots may exhibit some of these behaviors at other times that may not indicate aggression specifically. For example, a parrot may pin his eyes when quite excited or playing. It is important to look at the combination of behaviors and also the circumstance that is eliciting the responses to accurately conclude aggression is occurring. The best way to improve the companion parrot owner's ability to notice the subtle and not so subtle signs of aggressive behavior is to practice. It is helpful to watch your own bird, but also visit zoos and pet stores and observe the behavior of birds you do not know as well. It is a great opportunity to improve your ability to recognize the warning signs of aggression.

What Does Fear Look Like?

Another very important body language to be able to recognize is fear. This is important for several reasons. One reason is that when a fearful bird is forced to cope with what he fears, it can lead to an aggressive response. Therefore, recognizing fear in its early stages can prevent us from making choices that cause aggressive behavior. Another reason to avoid fear is that fear is an unpleasant experience for a bird. If that unpleasant experience is associated with the companion parrot owner, it can negatively effect the relationship between the parrot and the companion parrot owner.

Another important reason to avoid fear is that it is stressful. When stress-inducing events occur, fight or flight responses are exhibited. These fight or flight responses are associated with the first stage of stress defined by scientists as the alarm reaction stage. In this stage many physiological responses occur. This includes elevated corticosterone levels, increased heart rate, rapid breathing, elevated blood pressure, and more. Some birds, if exposed often enough to fearful events, can learn to acquiesce and/or tolerate the unpleasant experience. This occurs after a series of exposures to the stressful process or prolonged exposure to this type of stress. There is considerable research that shows the long-term detrimental effects of repeated exposure to uncontrollable aversive events with both animals and people.

Below are some of the warning signs a fearful bird may display. When these signals are observed, it is recommended that the companion parrot owner shift and adjust his or her behavior, or the conditions in the environment to reduce fear as much as possible.

Feather Position

A fearful bird needs to be streamlined and ready for flight. Remember when he feels backed into a corner, a bird must choose fight or flight. "Fight" would indicate aggressive behaviors are to follow. "Flight" means fear behaviors. Usually the first reaction a slightly fearful bird has is to lower all feathers and hold them in tight to the body in preparation for flight. Fluffed feathers are usually not associated with a fear response.

Eyes

Once again the eyes can give a great deal of information about a bird's level of comfort. When frightened, a fearful bird will usually have his eyes open wide. The eyes are also alert and usually darting looks are observed. A darting look occurs when a bird is looking for an escape path. Usually a bird will quickly look all around for options of escape. If a specific object, person, animal, or item is the cause of the fear reaction, often a bird will either keep one eye on the thing in question

A parrot normally keeps his eyes on something that he fears. Additionally, a fearful bird will keep his eyes open wide and look for an escape route. Eye pinning is not associated with fear.

while continuing to look for an escape path or the bird will quickly look at the object and then quickly look for escape options. Eye pinning is not associated with a fear response.

Vocalizations

As described in the section on behavior in the wild, an alarm call is a very natural behavior for a parrot. In the early stages of a fear response a bird may simply appear quite alert, but once clear and present danger has been detected it is quite possible a parrot may give an alarm call. As mentioned in the ethogram, vocalizations of parrots sound very different. An alarm call sounds quite different from a contact call or the call of a parrot that has learned screaming will get a desired response. An alarm call indicates something quite frightening has occurred or is occurring. While it may not be advisable to respond to a parrot screaming for attention, responding to an alarm call can be comforting to a frightened parrot. Remember there is safety in numbers if you are a parrot out in the wild. By responding to the alarm call, a companion parrot owner can address the biological need of a parrot to feel safe from danger.

My own blue-fronted Amazon parrot reacts apparently instinctively to the sound of the cry of a bird of prey. Even the sound of a hawk scream on the television will cause my bird to stretch up tall, slick down his feathers, and look around as if alerted to danger. Wild bird calls of other species of birds, such a grackles and jays, outside the window also can cause a similar reaction. My response to such sounds can effect my bird's level of comfort immensely in these situations.

Other vocalizations can be small honks or barks that are usually exhibited by a bird that is facing almost certain capture and/or restraint. These sounds are usually not very loud and almost always occur in a very extreme state of fear for a parrot.

Mouth

When initially frightened the mouth of a bird may be opened slightly. This may increase, especially if a bird is being forced into an unpleasant situation and the behavior begins to change from fear to fear-induced aggression.

Breathing

Breathing at first may be very quiet, as a bird tries not to draw attention to himself. Breathing may become more rapid as fear intensifies.

Head Position

As mentioned in the section describing eye movements, the head may move rapidly as the bird looks in many directions for a way to avoid the fearful experience. Head movements can be quite rapid and are usually directed away from the thing the bird fears. In general a bird that is fearful will choose to move away from what he fears. A bird that is aggressive may move towards the object or person in question.

Wing position and movement

The wings of a fearful bird are initially tight to the body. As a bird becomes more frightened, the wings are held out to the side as the bird prepares to fly away. Often this is accompanied by a springing motion, in which the bird performs quick "knee bends." In this position the bird looks as if he would leap into the air at any moment. If a bird can move away from what he fears, he will. This may mean walking or flying away. Sometimes birds will perform repetitive escape motions in desperation. For example, a bird may cling to the side of the cage and repeatedly grasp at the bars with the feet and beak as if climbing away. A very desperate bird may even turn over his back and present his feet. Again these occur in the very latter stages of fear. It is highly recommended to recognize and respond to the more subtle signals that indicate fear.

Almost any desired behavior can be achieved without ever creating a fear response in your companion parrot. By being sensitive to fear and aggressive behavior, companion parrot owners can develop a wonderful relationship with their birds based on mutual trust. A bird that trusts that his owner will not do anything that the bird does not like is less likely to have a reason to bite or behave otherwise aggressively. Subsequent sections will describe how to teach a bird to present desired behaviors while avoiding fear and aggression.

Chapter 6

Parrots and Punishment:
Methods That Are Least Recommended for Modifying Aggression

People are familiar with the use of punishment as a means to modify human behavior. In human culture, people have used spankings, yelling, removal of privileges, isolation, food deprivation, and other punishments as accepted means of teaching an individual something they did was wrong. And at times these methods successfully change unwanted behavior. It makes sense that we would naturally try to use punishment to modify behavior we do not like in our companion animals. A closer look at what punishment is and how it works may help demonstrate why, in general, punishment is not the best choice for modifying a parrot's unwanted behavior.

Punishment really is a very specific behavior modification concept. It also follows specific rules. A definition provided by Dr. Susan Friedman states that punishment is the presentation of an aversive stimulus, or removal of a positive reinforcer, that serves to decrease or suppress the frequency of the behavior. The use of punishment tends to produce detrimental side effects such as counter aggression, escape behavior, apathy, and fear. Also, punishment doesn't teach the learner what to do to earn positive reinforcement. Many times punishment is delivered

The use of punishment tends to produce detrimental side effects such as counter aggression, escape behavior, apathy, and fear.

minutes, hours, or days after the unwanted behavior occurred. It is difficult for an animal to then make the connection that the punishment had to do with a behavior he did in the past. Parrots are focused on the present. The timing of the punishment will determine what behavior punishment might possibly effect.

For example, perhaps you come home to find your parrot has freed himself from his cage and is now sitting calmly on top of it. You look around the room and notice your escape artist has destroyed the base of your antique grandfather's clock! No doubt, your ears are red with anger and your gut tells you your little feathered angel is in big trouble. You may want to yell at your bird, abruptly put him in the cage, perhaps cover him up, etc. Unfortunately none of these actions will change the condition of the clock. It also will not prevent your bird from chewing on the clock again in the future. In the bird's mind, he was just sitting there quietly and calmly and his crazy owner came home and freaked out at him for no apparent reason.

Not only is punishment not usually effective when working with parrots, but it can also greatly damage your relationship with your bird. Your parrot is likely to associate you with the unpleasant experience of the punishment.

Remember, punishment is usually something the animal does not like. This means that another drawback to punishment is that the unpleasant part of the punishment is usually associated with the companion parrot owner. In other words, the companion parrot owner gets to be the "bad guy." This can have a lasting negative impact on the relationship between the companion parrot and the companion parrot owner. When asked to choose the adults with whom they wished to interact, children generally chose the adults who had been associated with positive reinforcement. They generally did not select the adults that had been associated with the delivery of punishment.

Another disheartening factor about punishment is that there is a tendency for punishment to escalate. This is often because animals will choose to perform the behavior even in the presence of low levels of punishment if the positive reinforcement value is great. What this means is that often, because punishment is not as effective as other means of behavior modification, the punisher tends to try even harsher punishment to get desired behavior. This can lead to some very unfortunate situations. As the punisher becomes frustrated, the one being punished learns to be even more fearful of the punisher, or sometimes shuts down completely. In addition, punishment can sometimes cause an animal to try to escape or be even more aggressive as he looks for his own alternatives to stop the punishment from occurring. This has the potential to be a vicious cycle with unpleasant outcomes.

One of the worst drawbacks in using punishment to try to modify behavior is that an animal can learn how to exinguish body language that indicates aggressive behavior is about to follow. This is because the bird learns that presenting aggressive body language does not produce desired results. Therefore, there is no need to expend energy to present that body language. Instead, the bird may go straight to the behavior that will produce desired results, such as a well placed bite. Once a companion owner has lost the warning signs of aggression, it is a very precarious situation. Such an example can be seen in the parrot that steps up with no indication of aggression and then immediately bites the

To many parrots, yelling is fun. This means your bird doesn't see yelling as punishment, but views it as positive reinforcement. Yelling at him may encourage him to perform the unwanted behavior.

Who's the Boss?

Does your bird need to know you are the boss? This approach has been around for quite a while. Humans apply this to humans all the time as well as to other animal species. There is a notion that the animal has attempted to deceive or get away with something, and by dominating him, we can put the animal in his place. Remember that whatever the animal has done wrong, it probably had some positively reinforcing value to it. Chewing on the clock was fun for the bird! It wasn't a nasty trick he played on you. In fact, it probably had nothing to do with you at all.

Dominating an animal also assumes that the animal has an understanding of authority or some type of hierarchy (see sidebar on height and dominance). This is probably not the case with parrots. So why does dominating an animal seem to work at times? What usually happens in this situation is that the human will either punish or use force/negative reinforcement to get desired behavior. In many cases, the person is able to get compliance from the bird. This is because negative reinforcement does work. In a nutshell, it teaches the bird to do as the person says or else something bad will happen. Again, although the person may get behavior, the main drawback is that the bird has learned to associate negative experiences with the person. Thad Lacinak, V.P. Corporate Curator of Animal Training for the Seaworld and Bush Gardens Parks, made an important statement during a presentation on aggression he gave in 2004. He said, "Your job is not to get animals to do things for you, but to get them to like you." I found this to be one of the most important pieces of training advice I'd heard. Imagine trying to use domination as a means to train animals that can seriously hurt you, such as killer whales, tigers, or elephants. This is not to say such methods have not been used with large animals in animal training history, but in many circumstances that training style has lead to tragic encounters when an animal has had enough. Good trainers focus on positive methods. Give your bird the respect you might give a killer whale!

hand on which he sits. It is scary to be interacting with a bird whose communication is hidden or unclear.

Punishment is also less effective if it only occurs occasionally in conjunction with the unwanted behavior. In addition, if there is a reduction in unwanted behavior and the punishment is withdrawn, the unwanted behavior may return. This again demonstrates the less than desirable outcome that can occur when punishment is used as the only means to reduce undesired behavior.

Below are some examples of types of punishments sometimes used with companion parrots and explanations as to why they may not be effective at changing behavior:

Dirty Looks

Will giving your bird a disapproving look teach him to behave when he has done something wrong? This is another concept that is commonly used with people. People usually don't like a disapproving look because it means the person giving the look is not pleased with them. To humans, approval and acceptance, especially by those with power or authority, are usually important. The disapproving look may also mean something we dislike even more may come after the look. In other words, it is a form of punishment and a signal that an escalation in punishment may occur. What makes this form of punishment less effective is that in many cases birds are not that concerned with our approval. They may enjoy our attention and do things to get our attention, but this is different from seeking approval. Like any form of punishment, it is most likely to be effective if it is backed up with something the bird does not like and is timed to occur immediately in conjunction with the unwanted behavior. Keep in mind it is better to set your bird up for success, rather than setting him up to be punished. Other means of behavior modification can be more effective.

Hitting

I personally cannot think of a situation when it would be acceptable or necessary to hit a companion parrot. It often does not change the behavior, and the bird associates a strong negative experience with the person doing the hitting.

Yelling

Much like hitting, yelling usually does not do much to modify unwanted behavior. One reason is the bird's perception of yelling. To some birds, yelling may be fun. Parrots can be quite noisy. In some cases this may be perceived as positive reinforcement for whatever they were doing just prior to or during the yelling. For other birds, yelling may simply have no meaning. Our words or actions only have significance to the bird when there is reinforcement value associated with them.

For example, let's say your bird found your yelling to be very unpleasant because during the yelling process the bird had to endure some horrific garlic breath. In this case yelling could be considered punishing if the bird decreased screaming in response to your foul breath. (Because of parrots' poor sense of smell, perhaps that is a bad example; you get the picture.) Back up your yelling with something the bird perceives as negative and your bird may learn that yelling means bad things are about to happen. This means negative things are associated with the person doing the yelling.

Saying "No Bite" or "No"

Saying "no" to your bird in some ways is the same as yelling. "No" has meaning to humans, but for your bird it only has meaning if we teach the bird that it means something the bird does not like is to follow. I am sure many people have observed the child (or parrot) that completely ignores a parent repeatedly saying "no." This occurs because the word "no" by itself has no value or significance in this situation. We can back up "no" with an aversive, but again this associates an unpleasant experience with the person administering the aversive. Another kinder strategy is to teach a bird that a gentle "no" is a cue to discontinue whatever activity the bird is doing and sit calmly or return to you for positive reinforcement.

Shaking a Finger

Once again this is something that means something very specific to humans. To humans, we have learned to equate the finger shake with "no." However, it doesn't necessarily mean anything to a bird unless we teach the bird it means something. Some birds may think a finger waved in front of their faces is interesting and perhaps a toy. Some may dislike something moving close to their faces and attempt to bite at it. It is unlikely a bird understands that this means to stop doing whatever it is you are doing or what you have just done is unacceptable. This is different, of course, if the finger shake is perceived as unpleasant by the bird or followed by another unpleasant experience.

Beak Grabbing and Shaking

Much like the finger shake, this also depends on the perception of this experience by the bird. Some may think having their beak grabbed is a form of play. Some may think it is an invitation for sexual behaviors, such as regurgitation. Others may respond by trying to bite the hand that moves quickly for their beak. Some may be startled and/or fearful. Like

Some birds think of having their beaks shaken as a form of play, and it will frighten other birds. Using beak shaking as a form of punishment is rarely effective at modifying behavior.

other forms of punishment, it can work but there are better ways to modify behavior.

Dropping the Bird

One natural response to being bit by a parrot is to drop the bird. This is understandable as a bite can be quite painful. In some ways, this is helpful in that the bird is no longer on your person and able to continue biting. Also, if the bird is on the floor, their natural instinct to be elevated creates a desire for the bird to step up on the person it just bit. Because the bird would prefer to be off of the floor, this allows the person to be associated with the positive reinforcement of providing the bird a means to be elevated. So, in some ways this can help create a positive interaction with the person. Gently putting the bird on the floor may be helpful during or immediately after a bite, but ultimately it is far more successful to avoid the situation that created a need for the bird to bite in the first place. Therefore, although gently putting the bird on the floor may be more acceptable than most actions, consider prevention first. We will explore the concept of prevention more in following chapters.

Does Your Bird Need to Be Covered at Night?

For many, many years it has been an accepted practice to cover the bird's cage at night. While there can be value in this for some birds, it important to note that this is not always a good choice for every bird. Usually an extremely nervous bird may become calm with less visual stimuli. Many birds prefer the opportunity to see what is happening in their environment. In some cases a night light can offer more comfort as it allows a bird to see what may be causing suspicious noises in the night. It can also help prevent a bird from hurting himself by flying into the sides of his cage or other obstacles if frightened during the night. If you decide to cover your bird's cage, keep in mind the act of putting the material over the cage can be very frightening to a bird. This should be done slowly and carefully to avoid scaring the bird. If a bird is too nervous to allow the cover to be placed, perhaps it is best left off of the cage.

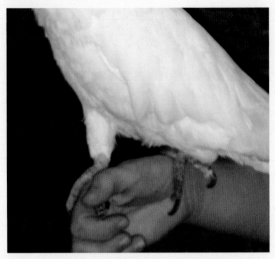

Toe pinching is sometimes recommended as a punishment, but, like other forms of punishment, it has drawbacks. Additionally, toe pinching may cause or worsen aggression and may damage the bird/owner relationship.

Pinching a Bird's Toe

Typically a bird does not like to have his toe pinched, so in this case there is no question of what the animal's perception of this action is. We can be relatively confident the bird will not like it. The problem is that the companion owner is the one doing the pinching. Once again this associates a negative experience with the companion. In addition, a bird may respond by biting at the fingers that are pinching his toes. The pinching can cause or worsen aggressive behavior.

Squirting the Face With Water

This is another relatively popular method used to punish birds for bad behavior. Again, this may have limited success because some birds may see this as an invitation for a nice shower. Others may find it aversive, and, of course, those birds will associate the owner with the squirting. There is also the potential for the completely confused bird. This can happen when sometimes the squirt bottle is used as punishment and sometimes the squirt bottle is used for a bath. This can create a bird that is unsure what to expect when the squirt bottle appears. Whatever meaning the squirt bottle has is extremely diluted, because the usage is inconsistent.

Putting the Bird in a Box

One unusual method described to me by a client was called "boxing." The breeder from whom she acquired the bird recommended whenever her bird screamed to grab the bird and put him in a cardboard box. To me, this method would be extremely damaging to the relationship between the companion parrot owner and the bird. This is because the first thing that happens after the bird screams is that the owner grabs the bird. Therefore, the owner becomes a terrifying person to the bird, even more so, when the owner then forces the bird into a cardboard box.

Putting the Bird Back in His Cage

Another type of punishment that is less harmful and can sometimes be effective is to put the bird back in his cage. It is more likely to be effective when the timing is directly connected to the unwanted behavior. The other element that is important is that the bird must view going back in the cage as something he does not want to do *at that time*. An unfortunate drawback to working with a bird that does not want to go back into his cage is that sometimes the bird can learn to bite to avoid going back in the cage. Therefore, while at times this can be helpful, ultimately it again demonstrates how challenging it can be to use punishment as a means to modify parrot behavior.

Time-outs: the Acceptable Punishment

One form of punishment that is considered acceptable in the world of animal training is a time out from positive reinforcement, or simply timeout for short. Before anyone places their bird on a chair facing the corner, perhaps a little clarification is in order. A time-out when training animals is as simple as the trainer discontinuing interacting with the animal. This may mean the trainer walks away from the animal, turns his or her back on the animal, and/or simply doesn't look at the animal. This type of time-out may last just a few seconds. The idea is that in those seconds or

Does Your Bird Know What He Is Saying?

It is uncanny how parrots seem to know how to say the right things at the right times. I know many parrots that say "hello" when the phone rings, or bark like the dog when there is a knock on the door, or say "goodbye" as you are heading off to work. It certainly seems that they know what they are talking about. While it is without question that parrots are remarkably intelligent, it is important to remember that they have learned what they have been taught. For example, I once worked with second-hand scarlet macaw named Sam. Whenever a hand was presented to him to step up, he would say "step up" and then promptly bit. It was clear to me he had probably been trained to step up in the past via negative reinforcement. I eventually taught him to step up on the hand for positive reinforcement, but never used the verbal cue step up. My only cue was the presentation of my hand. What I noticed happening is that whenever something Sam did not like was occurring and he was about to bite he said, "step up!" Sam learned that "step up" means bite! Therefore the meaning of the words "step up" for Sam was much different than our human interpretation. Birds learn to say words and associate them with certain circumstances. It may not mean they understand the human interpretation of the words, but they certainly understand the circumstances in which to use those words.

African grey parrots are famous for their ability to talk and seemingly use words in proper context. Many parrots have learned to use words in an appropriate manner, such as saying hello when the phone rings

Putting your parrot back in his cage can be effective at modifying his behavior only if he doesn't want go there at that time. If he wants to go back to his cage or generally enjoys being there, putting him in the cage can actually reinforce bad behavior.

moments the animal learns that whatever he did just prior to the time-out caused the animal to lose the opportunity to get the positive reinforcement he was receiving from the trainer. That positive reinforcement could be food, play, attention, touch, etc. Therefore, in order for the time-out to be effective, it must occur directly after or during the undesired behavior and the animal must want the positive reinforcement. Basically it teaches the animal that undesired behavior causes him to miss out on all the fun. This type of punishment, when paired with other training tools such as positive reinforcement, can be useful in communicating to an animal what behavior is desired. Therefore, the correct application of a time-out is critical to its success as a teaching tool. Of all the types of punishment, this is considered acceptable because it does not involve the application of an aversive.

Here is an example of how one might use a time-out to get desired behavior. Picture a macaw sitting on a perch. Jeff would like the macaw to step up on his hand. This macaw has stepped up on Jeff's hand many times in the past and has received a peanut when he does the behavior.

One acceptable and effective type of punishment is the time-out, meaning that you stop interacting with your bird and ignore him for a few minutes. Your bird will learn that these time-outs are lost chances to earn rewards.

Therefore, the macaw understands that he will be positively reinforced for stepping up. Jeff presents his hand in front of the bird's body. Instead of stepping up, the bird lunges at the hand with his beak. Jeff then collects his peanuts and walks away. He returns in two minutes and offers his hand again. This time the bird steps up and receives a peanut. Over time, if this scenario is repeated, the bird will learn that lunging at the hand causes Jeff and the peanuts to go away. This can lead to a bird that steps up immediately when asked.

Punishment (except for time-outs) in general is usually not the preferred behavior modification tool of professional animal trainers. Keep in mind that the path to good behavior can be created without the use of aversive types of punishment. Practice avoiding the use of punishment and focus on utilizing positive methods to get the behavior you want. This can be challenging at first. You may have to really concentrate to prevent yourself from using punishment. If you are really angry, walk away from the situation if at all possible. Come back and interact with your bird after you have had time to think through the situation and determine an acceptable way to create good behavior.

Chapter 7

Tools and Techniques
To Address Problems
With Aggression

If you have read this far you have already completed an important step in solving aggression problems. You have gained an education on how aggression works and learned about the motivations behind aggressive behavior. You have also increased your sensitivity to what aggressive behavior looks like in its early stages. Now let's outline some specific actions you can take to address aggressive behavior.

Below is a list of ten strategies that can be utilized when dealing with an aggressive event. Following the list is a detailed explanation of how to apply these strategies. Each step is described separately, but you will notice that some combination of the steps is applicable in almost every aggression scenario. A few of the steps are more appropriate for specific situations or are perhaps less effective than some other steps. Evaluate the aggressive behavior you are trying to modify and choose which steps can be most helpful to address your situation. After the detailed descriptions of the steps, we will revisit the different types of aggression and look at the application of the steps for each category of aggression.

- Keep notes on aggressive behavior to help identify the cause of aggression.
- Avoid circumstances that elicit aggressive behavior.
- Do not attempt to "work through" aggression by ignoring aggressive behavior and continuing to work with the bird.
- Divert the attention.
- Do not accidentally reinforce aggressive behavior.
- Reinforce any behavior other than aggressive behavior.
- Teach cooperation with small approximations and positive reinforcement.
- Teach your bird to do behaviors that are incompatible with aggression.
- Use repetition of a simple behavior to reduce aggression.
- Put the aggression on cue, and then never ask for it.

Keep Notes on Aggressive Behavior

Often we are hurt or embarrassed when an aggressive incident occurs with our companion parrot. This is understandable because usually we love our companion parrots and we are trying to give them the best lives possible. It is easy to take the event and personalize it. In some cases we are embarrassed that the "love of our lives" would do such a thing that we try to cover up the incident. But covering up the events doesn't help us solve the problem.

I once read a book targeted at developing management skills. It was called *Getting Past No* by William Ury and Robert Fisher. One of my favorite pieces of advice I gained from this book was a concept the author called "Going to the Balcony." The idea is that whenever you find yourself in an unpleasant situation in which you might lose control of your emotions, you try to separate yourself. In other words, you go to the balcony and look down at the event that just occurred from a distance. Essentially you remove yourself emotionally from the situation. This is an excellent concept to apply after an aggressive interaction with a parrot. First, it gives you an opportunity to regain your composure and remind yourself not to resort to punishing techniques. It then allows you to ask yourself what actually happened. Ask yourself what type of aggression this might have been: territorial,

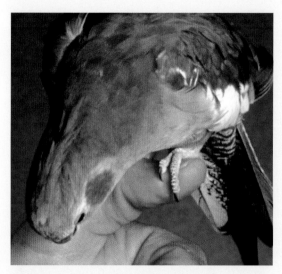

Keeping notes on your bird's aggressive behavior can help you determine exactly what circumstances cause your bird to be aggressive.

displaced, learned, etc.? Does this relate to behavior of parrots in the wild? What were you doing when the aggression occurred? Could you have done something different to avoid the aggression?

Keep a notebook on your bird's aggressive behavior. Document the answers to the questions above. Include the date, time of day, who was in the area, and your interpretation of what might have been going on in your bird's head before, during, and after the aggression occurred. By being open to acknowledging the specific details of the aggression, you are one step closer to solving the problem.

Here is an example of what aggression notebook might look like:

Snowball, Umbrella cockatoo

June 23, 2004

Time: 8:30 a.m.

Snowball was sitting on his T-perch outside of the cage. I needed to go to work, so he needed to go back into this cage. He stepped up onto my hand right away when I presented it. As I was walking towards his cage, he leaned over and bit my hand. He would not let go and I had to pry his beak off of my hand. I put him back on the T-perch while I cleaned my wounds. I then used a stick to put him back in the cage. After I put him in the cage he jumped and clung onto the wire like he wanted to come back out. I think he bit because he did not want to go back into his cage. Maybe he has learned if he bites me he will not have to go in the cage.

July 1st, 2004

Time: 6:30 p.m.

I was watching TV with Snowball on my leg. I was petting him. He was very relaxed. Tom came home and leaned over the back of the chair for a kiss hello. I looked up at Tom. In that moment, Snowball bit my arm. I jumped up which caused Snowball to end up on the couch. He then strutted around the couch with his crest up and vocalizing. After about 15 minutes, Tom went into the bedroom. Snowball was sitting on the edge of the couch preening. I sat down on the couch and Snowball crawled into my lap and solicited more petting. I think Snowball bit

If you keep a careful notebook of interactions with your bird, you should be able to identify patterns in his behavior.

Does Your Bird Need To Obey the "Step Up" Command?

Command, for me, is a difficult word to consider using when working with animals. To me it indicates a level of control or force. When I work with animals, I look at it as more of a relationship based on choice. If I use good training strategies, I hope a bird will choose to step up. Therefore, I never expect a bird to obey anything. I will present my hand to a bird and if he chooses to step up, I positively reinforce him. If the bird gives me body language that says he does not want to step up, I simply walk away and try again later. The bird does not have to step up. But what he will learn is that if he is slow to step up or chooses not to step up, he will miss out on the positive reinforcement I have to offer. In the long run, you create a bird who trusts that you will never force him to do something he does not want to. Eventually the bird will step up quite readily once he understands every time he does choose to step up, good things happen.

This person is using positive reinforcement to teach her bird to step up. Parrots are intelligent and quickly learn that performing this behavior leads to a reward.

because he did not want Tom to be so close to me and him. Maybe Snowball is bonded to me and redirected aggression on me when Tom came too close. Or maybe he thinks the couch is his territory and Tom is not allowed in his territory, so he showed his dissatisfaction by displacing aggression on me.

August 19, 2004

Time 2:15 p.m.

My brother, Mark, came to visit for the week. Snowball was letting him pet his head through the bars. I was watching. He seemed okay with Mark, so we thought maybe he would step up onto Mark's hand. Mark put his hand in the cage and in front of Snowball. Snowball looked at his hand and then bit it. He did not bite too hard. But it scared Mark and he withdrew his hand. Mark tried petting him again through the bars of the cage and Snowball seemed fine. I think maybe having Mark try to pick up Snowball was more than Snowball was ready to do. Snowball also did not show any body language that would indicate he was going to step up. Maybe Mark should have removed his hand earlier since Snowball did not want to step up. I think he bit to say he did not like the hand there and did not want to step up.

The wonderful thing about keeping notes on behavior is that patterns can begin to emerge. You may notice that your bird seems to exhibit more territorial aggression during certain times of the year. You may also notice certain similarities in aggressive events. You may notice repetition of aggressive behavior in certain circumstances. Even the act of forcing yourself to sit down, think about the situation, and then write about it can offer new insights into what occurred. Keep your aggression journal handy. It will be an important tool for solving the problems.

Avoid Circumstances That Elicit Aggression

To me, this is like the old joke that says, "Doctor, my arm hurts when I go like this. What should I do?" And the doctor says, "Don't move your arm like that." One of the best ways to solve aggression is to avoid doing things that cause aggression. For example, look at the three entries for Snowball's aggression journal.

In the first example, Snowball did not want to go back in the cage. There are several strategies one could use to avoid aggression in this situation. The owner could leave the bird in the cage in the morning, leave the bird on the T-perch, move the T-perch over to the cage and let the bird crawl in, use a stick to move the bird, or—my personal favorite—train the bird to go back into the cage for positive reinforcement.

In the second example, the aggression also could have been avoided. Here are some strategies that could have helped: The owner could have asked Tom to wait until she put Snowball away before he came near to her; the owner could have put the bird in the cage just prior to Tom coming home; the owner could have positively reinforced Snowball with a peanut for remaining calm when Tom approached; the owner could plan to spend time with Snowball when she is sure no one will come too close.

In the third example, the aggression is directly related to the hand coming up to the bird. Obviously, the easy strategy is not to have Mark put his hand in the cage. However, perhaps the family wants the bird to step up on to new people. In this case, I would focus on training the bird to step up on to new people for positive reinforcement. While the bird is still learning to do this, I would recommend new people do not present their hand to the bird. Once the bird has learned this behavior and you have fully explained to the person in question what to do, then it more likely Snowball will step up without aggression.

When trying to avoid doing things that may cause aggressive behavior, it is important to be sensitive to your bird's behaviors. This is when reading and interpreting bird body language is critical. Remember birds give many subtle signals that indicate aggression well before they are going to bite. Look for those signals. Note them in your aggression logbook and be aware when they happen. This is your communication that you are heading down the road to serious aggression. Pay attention to those signals and stop what you are doing before you get to the point at which the bird is going to bite. This will be essential to helping you learn to avoid aggression before it happens.

Rehearsal of aggression is a concept that says the more an animal practices aggressive behaviors, the more likely you are going to perpetuate aggressive behavior. Therefore, the more your companion parrot learns to use his repertoire of aggressive behaviors, the better he gets at aggression. In other words, practice makes perfect. In addition, studies have shown that when an aggressor is confronting an individual that cannot retaliate, he or she may escalate the severity and frequency of attacks. This is another excellent reason to focus on preventative measures. To avoid rehearsal of aggression, do whatever you can to avoid circumstances that elicit aggression in your bird. Letting an animal "get it out of their system" only leads to more fighting.

This strategy of avoiding aggression is something that should be applied to all aggression scenarios. Start paying attention to what actions encourage aggression and discontinue doing them. In other words, set your bird up for success by not contributing to the cause of aggressive behavior.

Do Not Attempt to "Work Through" Aggression

Working through aggression means the person continues doing what was causing the aggression and attempts to modify the animal's aggressive behavior via punishment and/or negative reinforcement. This is a classic mistake many trainers and companion parrot owners

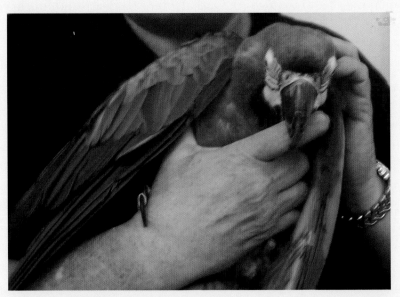

Avoid having a battle of wills with your bird. This will not solve the problem and can cause aggression to escalate.

make. Perhaps it ties back to the notion that we are in control of animals. The goal is not to be in control or dominant over an animal, but to create a working partnership based on clear communication and positive reinforcement.

Working through aggression can lead to all the drawbacks associated with punishment and more. These drawbacks include the following:

- More aggression (rehearsal of aggressive behavior)
- Escalation of aggressive behavior
- Fear
- Fleeing or an attempt to escape from the punishment
- Negative experience associated with the person
- Escalation of punishment
- Complete shutdown of behavior from animal
- Animal refuses to participate
- No resolution of aggression problem

When you see aggressive behavior, make note of the circumstance and then back out of the situation. You will not help or solve the problem by forging ahead into a battle of wills with your bird.

Divert the Attention

While it is important to do our best to avoid aggressive behavior, the small warning signs an animal gives us are the precursors to larger aggressive actions. Seeing the warning signs can be a good indicator that it would be best to back out of the situation. Sometimes leaving the scene may not be an option. In those situations, trying to divert the attention of the animal toward something else can get the animal's mind off of aggressing and allow a window of opportunity to open up and apply some of the recommendations in upcoming sections.

Diverting attention is different from positively reinforcing aggression. For example, we do not want to reinforce aggression by perhaps diverting attention with a toy which may have a positive reinforcement history for the bird. There are other means to distract a bird that can be used. Consider the following application of this strategy.

Some aggression is about location, such as territorial aggression. The bird's aggressive behavior has very much to do with his location.

One strategy for overcoming aggression is to divert your bird's attention by changing rooms or moving him. This gives your bird a new set of surroundings to pay attention to, rather than paying attention to whatever was causing his aggressive response.

Certainly in this situation it makes sense to remove the bird from the territory. It would be reasonable to assume the aggression will lessen. This certainly can and usually does happen. Changing the environment can also be helpful in other aggression scenarios.

Birds by nature are relatively sensitive creatures. Parrots are quite alert to changes in the environment. Small changes, and large for that matter, can be important to note for survival. Because of this, a change in environment can be helpful redirecting a bird's attention from aggression to his environment or other distractions. This is more applicable to certain types of aggression than others. For example, if you have a bird that becomes extremely excited or "pumped up" simply walking into another room he has never seen may cause him to switch from excited to alert. In essence, we are redirecting this bird's attention to other, perhaps more important matters. Therefore, a change of environment can sometimes be a helpful tool when managing aggressive behavior. Keep in mind this is only a tool to use for a quick redirection of focus. Moving a bird to a new location and leaving him there is not the same strategy. Leaving a bird in a new location will eventually result in the bird acclimating to the new environment. When this happens, it is likely the same aggression problems will reoccur once the bird has become comfortable in his new location.

Change Is Scary!

Parrots are sensitive creatures. New things, new people, new environments, even new food can sometimes cause a bird to be fearful or otherwise suffer stress. This sensitivity to change and to novel things most likely has to do with survival. When an animal in the wild is a potential prey item, it is wise to be wary. Some parrot species are more sensitive than others. Some of this can be due to innate characteristics of the species, but parrots can be taught to be comfortable with change. The best opportunity to expose your bird to new things is when he is young. Most young parrots are quite malleable and open to change. This allows you the opportunity to let your bird experience something without the new circumstance causing fear. You then have the opportunity to positively reinforce your bird for being calm around a new thing or situation. As a bird matures, this openness tends to fade and a bird becomes more careful. But a bird that has had positive experiences with a circumstance early on is less likely to be nervous in future encounters. Older birds can also be desensitized to new things, but it can be more challenging. With an older bird it may be necessary to go very slowly so as not to evoke a fear response in your bird. Each small advance made towards allowing a new experience should be followed up with positive reinforcement. Eventually your bird will be more confident with change.

Do Not Accidentally Reinforce Aggressive Behavior

Usually, nobody wants to reinforce aggressive behavior, but sometimes it happens inadvertently. An obvious example is when a bird bites and the person offers the bird a treat after the bite in hopes that it will prevent more biting. This of course teaches the bird exactly the opposite. This teaches the bird that biting will result in a treat, so do it more often!

On the other hand, sometimes the reinforcement is not so obvious. For example, when Snowball bit his companion parrot owner when she tried to return him to the cage, she put Snowball back on the T-perch. This is a reasonable thing to do since she was probably in pain and just wanted to get the bird off of her hand. It was surmised that Snowball may have been biting because he did not want to go back to the cage. After he bit, he was returned to the perch. The biting worked! He got what he had hoped for. Therefore, he learned that biting when being returned to the cage will result in the positive reinforcement of getting to go back to the perch.

Giving your bird a toy to distract him or divert his attention can reinforce the negative behavior. He can learn that biting or other misbehavior will lead to him getting a toy to play with.

This is why trying to determine the bird's desired outcome for the aggressive behavior is very important. The action you choose to make after the bite has the potential to positively reinforce the action of biting. As in the example above, sometimes it is almost impossible to avoid reinforcing the behavior. For example, look at what happened when Mark presented his hand for Snowball to step up. Had he not withdrawn his hand and continued to force the bird to step up on the hand, it is likely Mark would have received a very serious bite. Instead, he chose to remove his hand after a gentle bite. Technically this reinforced the biting action. Snowball learned if he does not want to step up, bite the hand and it will go away. This doesn't mean Mark should have continued and accepted a serious bite. The ideal response would have been to look for other subtle signs that indicated the bird did not want to step up and refrain from trying at that time. Another option would be to use a peanut or treat to lure the bird onto the hand. The best choice is to train the bird using positive reinforcement to step up onto many different people.

Reinforce Any Behavior Other Than Aggressive Behavior

Reinforcing any behavior other than aggressive behavior is a great way to get in the habit of rewarding good behavior and ignoring bad behavior. This is something that the companion parrot owner can use whenever interacting with his or her bird. The idea is to make a clear distinction between good and bad by only reinforcing good behavior.

For example, remember the parrots in the sanctuary that had learned to bite hands rather than step up? Initially they would lunge at my hand when presented. One strategy I used in the process was to reward the birds for doing anything that was not aggressive while my hand was present. If they sat calmly, they received a sunflower seed. If they took a step towards me they received a sunflower seed. As long as they allowed the presence of my hand and did not behave aggressively they received positive reinforcement. In the beginning, I was not concerned if they actually stepped up onto my hand. I knew that was a few training sessions farther down the road. The first step was to help the birds learn that everything other than aggression would receive

A useful strategy is to reinforce any behavior that is not negative or aggressive. This can include simple behaviors an owner may take for granted, such as sitting on his perch.

positive reinforcement. This also helped the birds to experience more positive interactions with me and increase the odds they would look forward to my presence.

This method can teach a companion parrot owner to be very observant and also to remember to reinforce good behavior. It also opens the door to the many, many things a parrot might be doing that falls into the category of "good." Remember, humans often forget to note the positive and focus mostly when an animal misbehaves. Get in the habit of noticing good behavior by applying this strategy.

Teach Cooperation With Small Approximations

I mentioned earlier that training is just another word for teaching. I also mentioned training is also a form of communication. Training is a set of tools that allows people to explain to an animal what they want. Training itself could easily fill up an entire book. Here we will explore some of the basics and how they can help with aggression problems. The following is a brief description of some of the elements of training.

Cue: a signal that tells the animal what you want him to do. Many trainers use verbal and/or hand cues.

Bridge or **bridging stimulus**: a signal that indicates when an animal has done something correct. It bridges the gap in time between when the animal did something correct and when he will receive positive reinforcement. Some examples of bridges include clickers, whistles, the word *good*, a touch, etc.

Positive reinforcement: anything the animal likes and will work to gain. It increases the likelihood a behavior will be repeated.

Approximations: when looking at a desired behavior, it is possible to break it down into small steps. Each step must be learned before moving on to the next step. Eventually all the steps together lead up to the final desired behavior. For example training a bird to step onto a new person may require the following steps or approximations:

1. Sit comfortably on the trainer's arm with a new person five feet from bird.
2. Sit comfortably on the trainer's arm with a new person three feet from bird.
3. Sit comfortably on the trainer's arm with a new person right next to bird.
4. Sit comfortably on the trainer's arm and eat treats offered by new person.
5. Put one foot on arm of new person for a second.
6. Put one foot on arm of new person and leave it .
7. Put both feet on arm of new person for a second.
8. Put both feet on arm of new person and remain there comfortably.

Each approximation is followed with positive reinforcement, usually in the form of food treats. Food treats work especially well if the bird is not comfortable with new people. Remember attention as a reward—or food for that matter—only works if the bird wants it.

Training can be used to address a host of aggression problems. For example, as was mentioned before, Snowball can be trained to return to the cage for positive reinforcement. Snowball can also be trained to allow Tom to be close to his spouse. Snowball can also be trained to step up onto new people. Birds that are aggressive because they are afraid can learn things are not scary when they are associated with positive

Can You Teach an Old Bird New Tricks?

I once worked with a 30-year-old hawk. This is extremely old for a hawk; however, at the time she was in good physical shape and flew like a champ in an educational program. I also had the opportunity to work with a 32-year-old Amazon parrot. At 32, this Amazon was no spring chicken, but he wasn't an old geezer (or should I say "gizzard") either. I started training him as part of a demonstration on how to train a parrot to allow nail trimming without restraint. He quickly learned to touch a target with his beak, hold his body in a specific position inside a cage and allow the nail trim. To me this was no surprise. In the wild, if animals do not learn from their experiences they are less likely to survive. Learning or the ability to learn does not stop because of age. In nature, it is likely the ones that have made it to an advanced age are the quickest learners. Sometimes our birds are waiting for us to be good teachers and show them what we want. Tap into your bird's potential, and your own by learning and applying some good training techniques. Your "untrainable" bird just might surprise you

reinforcement. Territorial birds can learn to allow others into their territory for positive reinforcement. All these behaviors can be learned while at the same time keeping birds calm and avoiding aggression.

Think about what you would like to see your bird do instead of display aggressive behavior. Try to think of steps or approximations you would take to get to that behavior. Spend time positively reinforcing your bird for accomplishing those steps.

Teach Your Bird Behaviors That Are Incompatible With Aggression

One way to help you decide what behaviors to train is to think of a behavior that is incompatible with aggression. In other words, while your bird is doing this behavior it would be impossible for him to be aggressive. While this may seem to be common sense, sometimes we forget we may actually have to teach an animal that it is worth his while to be calm in a certain circumstance. For example, if you teach a bird to sit on a particular perch away from you while you remove the food bowls, it would be impossible for the bird to bite you in this circumstance. Sitting on the perch away from you is incompatible with biting you.

To train this behavior you could begin by luring your bird to a certain perch in the cage with a peanut or other favorite treat. This can be done with the companion parrot owner offering the treat through the wire or the bars. When the bird just begins to make movement in the direction of the peanut, the companion parrot owner can say the word *station* or *perch* or whatever word is comfortable to use. A hand signal is also an option and can be used in conjunction with the verbal signal or separately. Just keep in mind this will eventually be the cue for the bird to move to this spot. Therefore, whatever word and/or hand signal that is chosen should be used consistently.

Teaching your bird behaviors that are incompatible with aggression—such as sitting quietly and calmly—is an effective technique. He'll quickly learn that sitting still earns him a reward.

Don't All Parrots Say, "Polly Wants a Cracker?"

Working with parrots in free flight bird show for years, I often found myself talking with guests after the show. Usually there was a bird by my side and usually someone would say, "Polly want a cracker?" to the parrot. It is fairly well-known that, in general, some species of parrots are more inclined to talk or mimic sounds than others (such as Amazon parrots and African grey parrots). Some species are also more inclined to copy whistling sounds (such as cockatiels). Of course, there are always exceptions. One incredibly proficient mimicking budgerigar can be seen on the video *Look Who's Talking* by Nature. This bird even quotes Shakespeare! To see even more fascinating information about bird vocalizations, invest in the BBC's *Life of Birds* video series. Parrots are not the only birds that mimic sound and this video shows some amazing examples.

Whether a bird will talk, whistle or both depends on the bird's inclination to copy sounds and training strategy. Not all birds mimic sounds. All parrots have the ability, but they don't all have the desire. You can help influence the desire by making sure good things happen in association with mimicking. For example, when you interact with your bird, repeat words or sounds you would like your bird to copy. You can positively reinforce any attempt your bird makes to mimic with attention or food treats. Once the bird understands the concept of getting reinforced for making sounds, he or she is more likely to attempt to vocalize.

The concept called "capturing" is used to put a vocal behavior on cue. This works after your parrot has already begun to mimic sounds on his own. The idea is that you catch your bird in the act of presenting the behavior you want as opposed to shaping it with small approximations. Here are the steps to put a vocal behavior on cue:

1. Listen for your bird to make a sound you want to put on cue. To avoid confusion, focus on capturing only one sound at time. Once the bird has learned one sound on cue, then try teaching a second.

2. The exact moment you hear the sound you want, use a bridge to tell your bird this is what you want. If your bird understands a bridge, this will be very helpful. You will be able to bridge the bird even if you are far away from it. Remember the bridge sound bridges the gap in time between when the bird did the behavior correctly and the offering of the positive reinforcement. This gives you time to walk from wherever you are to your bird if necessary.

3. Offer a treat or other positive reinforcement following the bridge.
4. Repeat steps 1–3 until your bird is offering the sound often.
5. Pick a cue to use to signal the bird to make the sound.
6. When your bird is making the sound often, you can usually slip in the cue right before the bird offers the sound. Offer lots of positive reinforcement when the bird makes the sound right after the cue.
7. Phase out reinforcing the bird for offering the sound and only reinforce the bird when it makes the sound after the cue.

Repeating words or sounds to your bird can sometimes help a bird to learn to copy you. Also associating positive reinforcement with any talking behavior can help, but it is important to remember to love your parrot, whether he or she is a chatty Cathy or not.

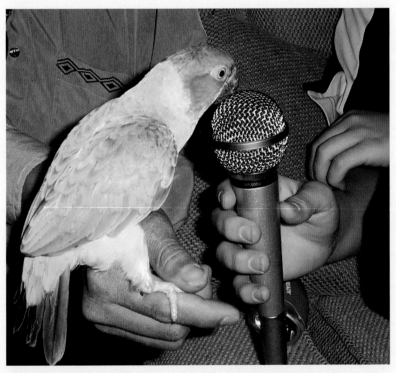

Capturing is the name for the process of teaching parrots to display natural behaviors, such as vocal mimicry, on cue.

Eventually the companion parrot owner fades out luring the bird to the perch with the peanut. This can be done by hiding the peanut in the hand. Once the bird arrives to the desired location, the companion parrot owner can use a bridge (such as the word *good*, or a click, or a whistle) to let the bird know he has completed the task correctly and reinforcement is to follow. After the bird hears the bridge, he can receive the peanut. In the beginning it is helpful if the bird receives the reinforcement very quickly after he hears the bridge. This helps the bird to learn the bridge means "treats are coming!" The behavior of stationing at a specific location is something a parrot can learn quite quickly as long as the bird has an interest in the treats.

Now when it is time to take out the food bowls, the companion parrot owner can give the cue. The bird goes to his designated location and receives his reinforcement. The bowls can be removed without causing aggression. If the bird starts to move toward the bowls before they are removed, the companion parrot owner can cue the bird again and reinforce him after he has returned to the proper location. The time the bird waits in the location before he receives reinforcement can be expanded by gradually adding a few more seconds to the time he sits at his station before he receives the bridge and reinforcement.

This is just one example of training a bird to present a behavior that is incompatible with aggression. There are many others scenarios to consider. For example, another idea might be to teach a bird to touch a target with his beak when a new person walks into the room. Or one could teach the bird to sit calmly when someone new enters the room. Initially, the bird may only be required to sit calmly for a few seconds before he is bridged and reinforced. Time is gradually added on to this so the companion parrot owner does not have to constantly put treats in the bird's mouth while a new person is in the room. It seems obvious, but sitting calmly while a new person enters the room is incompatible with being aggressive.

After you have reviewed your notes and determined what situations can cause aggressive behavior in your bird, think about incompatible behaviors you could teach your bird for those circumstances. Also, write down the steps or approximations you would need to make to train that behavior. One thing to keep in mind about approximations is that the bird may not achieve each step in one training session. This may occur over a period of days or weeks depending on the behavior. Work at a pace that allows your bird to fully grasp what you are trying to teach him. Make sure he has mastered one step before you move onto the next. Also remember if he has mastered a step to move forward in your training. Unless your bird is having trouble with a step, there is no need delay your progress.

The process of training an animal with approximations is like a dance between you and your bird. You may take a few steps forward, but if your bird is unsure, you may end up taking a step back. You may remain at this step for a little while and then you try to progress again. There is a constant shifting and adjusting to meet the capabilities of your bird at the time, but eventually you make more steps forward than you do backwards and your bird learns what you are trying to communicate. It is an intricate dance and one that I think makes training such an interesting field of study. It challenges your skills and always keeps you thinking. Very rarely does training become boring. Each species, each individual, each behavior brings a new set of criteria to the table.

Perhaps the next example can illustrate this dance better. Many people have heard of a behavior called "the dollar bill routine." This is a behavior one sees in animal presentations. A guest is asked to hold a dollar bill out to his or her side and a bird flies to the guest, takes the dollar, and returns it to the trainer. Essentially this behavior is a retrieve. The bird is required to retrieve a dollar and place it is a specific location. Here is a more detailed explanation of the approximations to train a portion of this behavior and also a closer look at the areas in which trainer and bird are usually "dancing" their way towards the desired behavior.

1. Set the bird on a small perch (approximately one foot in length). This is to limit where the bird might choose to go.
2. Offer the bird a small washer or other small but heavy object. Usually birds will pick it up with their beaks out of curiosity. If the bird will not pick it up, try hiding a piece of food behind the washer so the bird must touch the washer with his beak. Bridge and reinforce when the bird does this. (Continue shaping touching the washer until the bird picks it up.)

3. Hold a small bowl under the bird and eventually the bird will tire of the washer and drop it. Catch the washer in the bowl. Bridge and reinforce when the washer hits the bowl bottom.

4. Repeat this process several times.

5. After several repetitions, move the bowl over to the side slightly. The bird will probably not drop the washer in the bowl. If this happens, do not bridge or reinforce. Offer the washer again. Allow the bird to miss and not get reinforced one or two times.

6. Go back to trying to catch the washer in the bowl. Bridge and reinforce.

7. Try moving the bowl to the side again. If the bird gets the washer in the bowl, offer a large reinforcement. If not go back to step 3 and work up to step 5 again. Keep repeating this process until the bird understands the washer must go into the bowl in order to get the reinforcement.

8. Once the bird gets the concept that the washer goes into the bowl, start moving the bowl a little farther away. You will find you may have to go through steps 3 through 7 again. Eventually you will be able to hold the washer on one end of the perch and the bowl on the other.

9. Once this concept is understood by the bird, you can try switching the object to the dollar. When you do this go back to holding the bowl under the bird and catching the dollar. Gradually approximate the bowl farther away. This should go quickly this time.

Of course, there is more training to this behavior to have it ready for an animal presentation. The most challenging part is usually helping the bird to understand the object must go in the bowl. It also an excellent example of the intricate give and take involved in training a behavior.

Now let's get back to aggression!

Use Repetition of a Simple Behavior To Reduce Aggression

Another wonderful tool in addressing aggressive behavior is repetition. In general, parrots don't need a lot of repetition to learn something. They can learn quite quickly. Crows are quick learners too. For five years, I was part of a team presenting a bird demonstration at a famous theme park in Florida. One part of the show included the dollar bill routine. A pied crow was to fly out to a guest, retrieve a dollar bill, and return it to the presenter's pocket. Prior to flying to the guest, there was quite a bit of dialog. During this time, the crow was either on the arm of the presenter or standing on a rock. During an earlier part of the show, chicken feed sometimes accidentally got left behind in the grass on the stage. Unfortunately, this was discovered by the crow. This one incident of obtaining reinforcement (chicken feed) for hopping to the ground created a long term training challenge. Every time the crow came out on stage, it went foraging through the grass. Often the bird was reluctant to leave the tasty treats and return to the trainer. Fortunately, some good training strategies rectified the problem. This included calling the bird to the hand the exact moment the bird looked at the trainer and offering a huge jackpot of treats for coming when called. The point is that it only took one repetition to teach the bird to go to the ground and many sessions to get the bird back on track.

The previous example illustrates how one repetition can teach undesirable behavior. Now let's look at how many repetitions can reduce aggressive behaviors. To use repetition to reduce aggression it is helpful for your bird to already know how to do a simple behavior for positive reinforcement. This simple behavior can be stepping up on the hand or a stick, saying "hello," waving, or turning around. If your bird does not know a simple behavior, just the act of accepting a treat from you can work. I'll explain this in more detail.

The best time to use repetition is when you are interacting with your bird or are about to interact with your bird and you see the small signals that indicate your bird may do something more aggressive such as bite. It is in this moment that you can cue your bird to do the simple behavior he knows. Once he does the behavior, bridge and reinforce it with a treat. Immediately after the bird has finished his or her treat, ask the bird to do the behavior again followed by the bridge and reinforcement. Do the repetition as quickly as the bird will allow. What you will observe is that gradually the aggressive body language will subside as the bird becomes focused on the task at hand. Doing a behavior repetitively gets the bird's mind off of aggressing and onto other things. Repetitions also allow the bird to receive positive reinforcement in association with you, which can help improve the relationship. Repetition of a simple behavior he already knows makes it easy for the bird to do. This also allows you to positively reinforce the bird for good behavior instead of looking for ways to punish bad behavior.

In some cases a bird may be too aggressive or excited to present a behavior he knows on cue. In other cases he may not know a behavior on cue. In these situations you can just offer a treat from your hand. It is important to be very careful when offering a treat to a potentially aggressive bird. Here are some techniques you may use when trying this. Try using a piece of food that is long enough that when you hold it in your fingertips it extends half an inch or more beyond your fingertips. Slowly bring the food up toward the bird. Hold the food so that the bird has to reach for it and when he does get it, he can just barely reach the food, not your fingers. Hold the rest of your hand in a tight fist. When skin is taught, it is difficult for a bird to grab onto it. Do not use an open or flat hand to offer food. At first the bird, may lunge at the hand, or demonstrate some aggressive body language. Try to wait until he is slightly calmer and slowly offer the food at a safe distance. Once he gets the idea to take the treat, you can go quite rapidly. The more you practice this, the easier it gets.

Once you can do this comfortably, you can offer one treat right after another, as fast as your bird can eat it. Usually in just a few repetitions the bird's body language will shift from aggressive to "Hey, where are the treats?" Remember, using food treats only works if the bird wants the treat. If the bird has no interest in food, you may want to come back and try again later or with more preferred treats. This strategy requires careful observation and timing of the deliverance of the food reinforcement. Try to avoid offering reinforcement when the bird is showing high levels of aggressive behavior. The goal is to reinforce any glimmers of calm behavior.

Put the Aggression on Cue, and Then Never Ask for It

This final strategy for aggression is probably not one that I recommend as much as those previously mentioned. It is an interesting phenomenon that can work to some degree. In his book *Animal Training: Successful Animal Management Through Positive Reinforcement*, Ken Ramirez describes an example of training a dolphin to present a behavior called "jaw popping" on cue. Jaw popping is a behavior that dolphins will do that is an indicator of aggression. Training the behavior was not initially instigated as a means to address aggressive behavior, however, Ken and his staff observed that by putting the behavior on cue and then not cueing the animal for the behavior once it has been learned lead to a reduction in the dolphins exhibiting jaw popping.

We have already discussed different strategies for putting a behavior on cue. While this is a strategy that companion parrot owners may consider, I offer it more out of interest. An experienced trainer may find it an interesting angle to consider. The first nine techniques are much easier to apply and should lead to good success in reducing or eliminating aggressive behavior.

Chapter 8

Application of the Techniques
With the Different Types of Aggression

L et's look at the different types of aggression one more time and see where all these strategies can be applied to help avoid, reduce, or eliminate aggressive behavior. The first step in all cases is to identify the type of aggression in each occurrence. Utilizing the aggression logbook can help you identify the motivation.

Fear Aggression

Remember, a bird that resorts to aggression out of fear does so because he thinks he has no other option. Whatever is causing the bird to be fearful is not subsiding, so he aggresses as a desperate attempt to stop what is happening. The first step in stopping aggression in this type of situation is to discontinue doing whatever it is that is causing the bird to be fearful. This requires that the companion parrot owner be sensitive to the parrot's body language. The moment the bird shows any indication of fear is the moment things have gone too far.

The next step is to decide what it is you want your bird to do. Do you want your bird to step up? Do you want your bird to interact with a new toy? Do you want your bird to interact with strangers?

This cockatoo is afraid of the carrier and doesn't want to go inside. If he is forced to enter, he may resort to aggression in an attempt to avoid the situation.

Remember, you can pick a behavior that is incompatible with aggression. For example, stepping on the hand calmly is incompatible with biting the hand. This means you will need to spend time reinforcing calm behavior in the presence of the hand. Once you have identified what your goal is, decide what approximations or steps you will need to take to get that behavior trained. As you begin training, you will see that more repetitions will help increase the bird's confidence as he learns to associate positive reinforcement with the situation.

A fearful bird can be sensitive, especially if he has had a past negative experience with the behavior you want. The steps or approximations you decide to use may have to be very small at first. It is also very important that positive reinforcement happens after each step is achieved. Fearful birds can take longer to learn, but the end result is very rewarding.

Physical State-Induced Aggression

Conditions such a physical pain, illness, or exhaustion can sometimes lower a bird's tolerance for interaction and in turn lead to an

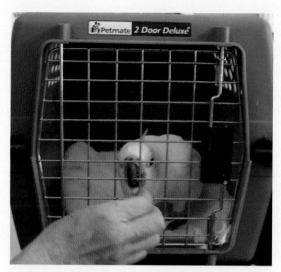

Positive reinforcement can overcome fear and fear-induced aggression. The cockatoo has now learned that being in the carrier does not harm him and that he will be rewarded for going inside.

aggressive response. Being observant of your bird's behavior will help you identify what may be causing the discomfort. Birds that are feeling localized pain will sometimes chew at the area that is irritating. You may also see a bird limping or drooping a wing in response to pain in those areas. Birds will also usually vocalize in response to pressure or touch on a painful area.

Most companion parrot owners have accidentally touched a pin feather and had a bird vocalize his displeasure. Pin feathers are new feathers that are still in the growth process. When a feather is growing in, it has a nerve and blood supply running through the shaft of the feather. The feather is also wrapped in a keratin sheath. This is what gives it the appearance of a stick or pin. When the feather is mature, the nerve and blood vessel retract. Once this happens the feather is no longer sensitive to touch, and the keratin sheath is usually ready to be removed by preening. If a bird vocalizes when a pin feather has been touched, it is because it hurts. It also means the feather is not ready to be preened just yet. The keratin sheath is required to protect the new feather for a bit more time. Parrots are clearly telling us "hands off that feather" in this situation.

Birds that are ill may be listless and inactive. They may not respond as they would normally in certain situations. Perhaps favorite toys or food items are no longer of interest. If your bird appears to be ill or in physical discomfort, make a visit to your avian veterinarian as soon as possible. Recognize that aggression in these cases is predictable. It will be helpful to your bird's condition to do your best to avoid aggravating whatever is bothering your bird if at all possible. This of course will help avoid aggression, but even more importantly, it will help your bird feel comfortable when he is obviously in need of special care.

One strategy that is applicable in this situation is to reinforce any calm behavior. This may help your bird feel more comfortable in general. However, your bird may not be receptive to treats or attention if not feeling well. If this is the case, then the extra attention may actually be more of an irritation than a positive reinforcement. Check to see how your bird is responding. Sometimes the best choice is to just give your bird some quiet time until he or she can be seen by the veterinarian.

A bird that is tired is not in need of medical attention, unless you suspect the lethargy is in connection to a health related problem. However, it is still a good idea to let your bird rest when he needs to. Rather than using training techniques to address aggression in these instances, the best choice is to avoid aggression by waiting for a moment when your bird will be more receptive to interacting. There will be plenty of other opportunities to interact with your bird.

Redirected Aggression

Redirected aggression occurs when something the bird does not like happens, and the bird acts out aggressively, usually on the closest thing. The most common scenario is when a parrot is bonded to one person in the household and another person walks up on that person and the bird when they are together. Typically the bird bites the person to whom he has bonded. In this situation your observation and notes are very helpful. You will quickly be able to identify situations in which your bird is more likely to present redirected aggression. You will have your best success by avoiding those circumstances. You can determine "safe" times of the day or circumstances to interact with your bird without the risk of someone walking up on you. You can create signals to let others in the household know you have the bird out and to give you warning if they need to come close to where you are.

You can also use training an incompatible behavior and/or reinforcing any behavior other than aggression to help reduce this type of aggression. You can keep a stash of treats in your pocket that you can use whenever you anticipate someone coming close to you. Reinforce the bird for sitting calmly before the aggression begins. If possible, try to have the person approach slowly. Have the person move away if any warning signs of aggressive behavior are observed. You can also cue your bird to perform repetitions of a simple behavior as a new person approaches. Remember, this will give the bird an activity on which to focus and allow him to receive positive reinforcement for good behavior in the presence of something he does not necessarily like. Keep in mind this unpleasant reaction to strangers coming close is based on some instinctual behavior of parrots. I recommend a great deal of emphasis be placed on avoiding circumstances that cause aggression in conjunction to utilizing training to prevent this type of aggression.

Territorial Aggression

A parrot needs a very good reason to want to let someone enter his or her territory. We can apply our strategies of avoiding aggression and training good behavior for positive reinforcement. One easy way to avoid aggression near the cage is to train the bird to come out of the cage on his own. This can be done by teaching the bird to crawl out onto a T-perch placed next to the cage. The T-perch can then be moved away from the cage to allow interaction with the bird away from the territory.

Another strategy is to teach the bird that whenever you enter his territory something good will happen. This may mean every time you walk by the cage you hand the bird a treat or drop a treat in the bird's food bowl. Soon the bird's response will change from aggression to anticipation whenever you enter the territory.

If your bird knows a behavior on cue, you can also cue your bird for that behavior whenever you plan to enter the territory. This allows the

If your bird exhibits territorial aggression inside his cage, you can train him to leave the cage voluntarily. This avoids the situation that causes him to respond aggressively.

bird to focus on something other than aggression and receive positive reinforcement from you for doing the behavior.

Possession Aggression

While a parrot can bite quite hard, usually humans are much stronger than parrots. Relatively speaking, it may not be too hard to wrestle an object out of a bird's beak. However, remember an important rule to reducing aggressive behavior is to avoid doing things that create aggressive behavior. It is not a wise strategy to get into a fight with your bird over an object. Instead focus on distracting and redirecting your bird's attention. For example, you can always hold a favorite treat out for your parrot to retrieve. As your parrot makes a move for the treat he will most likely drop whatever is in his mouth. You can then gently remove the object from the area while your parrot enjoys his treat. A treat is not the only thing that can be offered to redirect attention. Other interesting toys can be used as well. Better yet is to make sure the area in which your parrot will be is free of items that are off limits to curious

Wrestling your bird over an item can lead to him biting you and associating you with the unpleasant situation. It is more effective to use positive reinforcement to train him to drop items on cue.

parrots. This prevents the situation that may cause possession aggression in the first place.

You can also teach your bird to drop an item on cue. This falls into the training an incompatible behavior category. You can train this by holding another more interesting toy or a treat in front of your bird while he has another object in his mouth. Give your bird a cue, perhaps the word "drop." The moment he drops the object, bridge the bird, and offer him the alternative toy or treat. Eventually you can phase out showing the treat or toy and just use the verbal cue "drop." Then the next time your bird has something off limits in his mouth, you can cue him to drop the item and reinforce him for doing so. You will eliminate the need for a tug of war and potential aggression.

If your bird is demonstrating possession aggression in regard to his bowls, you can train your bird to station in a particular location as described earlier. You can also avoid aggression by simply removing your bird from the cage before you change the food bowls. This is another way to avoid setting you and your bird up for an aggressive interaction.

Excitement That Turns Into Aggression

Birds get excited about many different types of external stimuli. Your aggression logbook will be very helpful in identifying circumstances that cause a great deal of excitement in your bird. The best strategy to employ for this type of aggression is to avoid those situations. Some stimuli can be quite predictable. This includes when family members come home from school or work, when you are about to use noisy appliances, or when you play music. It is helpful to remember those moments may not be the best time to interact with your bird. Simply choose other times of the day for socializing with your bird.

However, some stimuli are less predictable. This includes things like the phone ringing, a knock on the door, or the dog barking. If you are able, sometimes the best choice in this situation is simply to place the bird off of you as quickly and gently as possible. Of course, it is also possible to train your bird to remain calm in those situations. You can recreate the situation in which you need your bird to be calm. For example, if your bird typically becomes "pumped up" when the phone rings, you and a friend can simulate this situation quite easily. One person will need to be with the bird. The other person will be responsible for two phones. One phone will be making calls; the other will be receiving calls. You may want to unplug other phones in the house on the same line. This gives you more control of how much stimuli the bird receives. Two cordless and/or cell phones work better, as it allows both phones to be gradually moved closer to the bird.

Depending on how excited your bird gets when the phone rings, you may want to begin with the phone and the bird far away from each other. Have the bird far enough away from the phone that when it rings it doesn't stimulate too much excitement. As the bird remains calm with the phone ringing, bridge and reinforce the bird. Gradually you can move the phone closer and continue bridging and reinforcing the bird for remaining calm. If the bird begins to get too excited, move the phone farther away and gradually work towards getting closer to the bird again. Once your bird has learned that calm behavior will be rewarded when the phone rings, you will be better prepared to avoid aggression in the future in this situation. It may be to your benefit to keep a stash of treats handy in your pocket or easily available in containers around the house. You can also gradually condition your bird to accept the companion parrot owner answering the phone and talking on the phone to the training. Introduce these elements gradually by only talking a little at first. Gradually introduce more conversation and volume. Reward your bird for remaining calm. If he is not calm you may have to reduce the volume and amount of talking to calm him and then gradually build up again. This is best trained in a simulated situation at first.

Despite our best training attempts, we are sometimes caught off guard. If by chance your bird is quite excited and you are all out of treats and toys, sometimes just moving to an unfamiliar location can redirect a bird's attention from excitement and possible aggression. This is because a bird's natural instinct to be wary of new things and new places usually causes the bird to suddenly switch from excitement to concern. It won't necessarily reduce aggression in the long term, but it can be a quick solution in some situations.

Rough play often leads to aggressive behavior. The best strategy is to avoid interactions that elicit aggressive responses. However, at the same time, most of us want to play with our parrot and both parrot and companion parrot owner seem to enjoy the interactions. One strategy that can be considered is to use objects/toys that are acceptable for your parrot to bite. A stuffed animal, a piece of wood, a rolled up towel are all objects that your bird can learn are acceptable for rough play. In addition if your bird redirects that rough play onto any part of your body, simply walk away from the interaction. Essentially you use a time out to teach your bird rough play with the identified objects is okay; rough play with your fingers is not.

Social Aggression

Aggression with other parrots can be very challenging to address. In some cases, there seems to be an instinctual drive to keep other birds away. This can be seen most commonly when the bird in question has bonded to another bird or person. There are some strategies that can be applied to attempt to bring the birds together. However, keep in mind it may not be possible to get some individuals to interact in a positive manner. Here are some strategies to apply.

Aggression between parrots is a challenging behavior to address. Parrots may not tolerate other parrots in their territories.

As mentioned in previous examples, a main goal will be to avoid aggressive interactions between the two birds. This means initially it is better to not place the birds in a situation in which they can actually touch or harm each other. The example described earlier in which two birds are howdied is a nice, safe way to see what two birds think of each other. Each bird can be placed in separate enclosure. The enclosures are then placed close together. The two birds can then be observed to see how they react to one another. Both birds can be offered treats for remaining calm in the presence of the other bird. Gradually the two cages can be moved closer if the birds seem to be behaving calmly.

One thing to keep in mind with this strategy is territorial behavior. If either or both of the birds display territorial aggression when in their cages, it may be beneficial to move both birds to two new enclosures in a different room. This can divert the attention from territorial aggression. After a few days, if both birds have not shown aggressive behavior towards one another, it may be possible to approximate the two birds interacting with one another outside of their enclosures. It is best to try this in an area that is not perceived to be the territory of either bird. Use a space large enough that either bird can leave the encounter if desired. Use two people to manage the birds. Provide lots of toys and treats as positive reinforcement for calm behavior in the presence of the other bird. You can also use other strategies such as reinforcing any behavior other than aggression and repetition of a simple behavior the birds already know.

Be very careful when introducing two birds to one another. The best candidates for a free contact introduction are ones that did not display any aggressive behavior towards one another while being howdied. If aggressive behavior was observed, it is very possible the two birds in question will not get along outside of an enclosure. Also consider size differences. While some mismatched birds will get along, remember a large bird could hurt a smaller one without much effort. Parrots can inflict some serious damage upon one another, and it can happen very quickly. Be aware there can be serious risks in allowing two birds to interact. Ask yourself how important it is for your bird to interact with another bird before you consider this strategy. Also, be prepared. Have a towel right by your side, if you have to intervene. Hopefully, a companion parrot owner's keen observations of behavior would prevent the need to use a towel to separate two birds, but it is wise to be ready for the worst case scenario if one chooses to attempt to introduce birds in this manner.

It is not always possible to overcome the aggression that can occur between two birds. At best, you may only be able to create a situation in which two birds are willing to tolerate each other's presence. If you see a substantial amount of aggressive behavior, you may want to reconsider the importance of having your bird interact with other birds. Some birds lead perfectly happy lives only interacting with humans.

Teaching a parrot to interact with new people can be many times easier than teaching a bird to interact with other parrots. That is because in this situation we have the ability to give clear directions to the humans. Just like in other examples, it is important not to force a bird to do anything. This can just lead to more aggression. Instead, it is important to pay attention to the signals that indicate a build up in aggression and use the strategies described to maintain the peace. When introducing a parrot to a new person, it is important to go slow,

These scarlet macaws are housed in enough space to escape aggression from their cagemates. In a home situation, giving birds this much room is impractical, so the owner must be careful when trying to keep parrots together.

reinforce calm behavior, or reinforce any behavior other than aggression. It can also be helpful to cue the bird for repetition of a simple behavior, such as touching a target, as a new person approaches. The new person can offer the treats to the bird so that the positive reinforcement is associated with the new person. Note that if a bird does not seem to like a new person, attention from that person is not positive reinforcement. Only when the bird views attention from that person as rewarding will it be a valid tool for that person. A companion parrot owner can decide what behavior is the final goal. Sitting calmly in the presence of new people? Stepping up onto new people? Interacting with new people? Once the ultimate goal is identified, it is then possible to decide the steps or approximations needed to get that behavior. Each day the companion parrot owner can try to work his or her way through the steps and offer positive reinforcement to the parrot as progress is made. By using good observation of the bird's body language to avoid aggression and using a process based on positive reinforcement, a bird can learn to accept other people in his life.

A bird that is bonded to one person will do better with a new person when the person to whom he is bonded is not around. Also, a bird that

Teaching a bird to interact with other people can be done without creating aggressive or fear behaviors by using positive reinforcement.

is territorial will do better if the interactions occur away from the bird's perceived territory.

You may recall that much of this type of aggression can be avoided if birds are exposed to many new people in association with positive reinforcement when they are young and more receptive to change. This is usually just about the time a bird would be fledging (beginning to learn to fly and then leave the nest) and for a short time after that.

Learned Aggression

As mentioned before, there are numerous examples of birds learning to be aggressive for a desired outcome. Unlike some other types of aggression, this type can be especially challenging because in the past, aggressive behavior in this circumstance allowed the bird to get whatever it was he wanted. In other words, it worked. For example, when Snowball bit his owner's hand as she approached the cage, he was allowed to remain outside of the cage. If aggressive behavior has resulted in the desired outcome more than once, it can be even more difficult to change. When birds have the opportunity to aggress, they will aggress more often. Practice teaches the bird that aggression is a good strategy for getting what he wants.

Using the steps outlined to reduce or eliminate aggression is a little more challenging to apply here. These situations will require companion parrot owners to be especially sensitive to reading and interpreting the bird's body language that indicates aggression, and also require that they apply good training strategy.

Let's walk through training Snowball to return to the cage without biting. By keeping an aggression logbook, we have discovered the aggression in this situation is learned aggression. We know one way to avoid the aggression in this case is to never put Snowball back in the cage. However, this is not practical. We can focus on training Snowball to present the incompatible behavior of entering the cage without biting. To train him we will need to identify the steps or approximations we will want to take to teach Snowball to enter the cage voluntarily. We also will avoid aggression by not asking for too much of Snowball too soon.

In this case, we want to reinforce calm behavior in Snowball while he sits on the hand. Gradually, we can move closer to the cage. As long as Snowball is calm, we can continue to reinforce him while he sits on the hand. Now here is where the challenging part enters the equation. If Snowball shows the slightest bit of aggression, we do not move ahead. We may even take a step farther away from the cage. This is where being extra sensitive to Snowball's body language is very important. Once he calms again, we can gradually move closer to the cage. Eventually Snowball will be in the cage, but perhaps reluctant to step off of the hand onto a perch. Remember this is a behavior that needs to be reinforced also. In the beginning, it may be necessary to lure Snowball onto the perch with a visible treat in one hand or in a bowl on the other side of the perch. Eventually we can fade out showing the treat to Snowball, and then hand it to him after he steps onto the perch. The first attempts at training this may be slow, but once Snowball understands he will be positively reinforced whenever he enters the cage, he will look forward to entering the cage and do so quickly and without aggression.

In cases of learned aggression, showing heightened sensitivity to your bird's body language will be helpful. Go slowly and recognize the tiniest signals that indicate aggression. Try to reinforce your bird before you see those signals and back off if you do. You may also need to use small approximations. This means you break the behavior down into very small steps. It may seem like you are constantly giving treats to your bird when you use small approximations. Eventually you will be able to allow greater intervals in between treats. In the end you will only need to use one treat to reinforce your bird after he completes the desired behavior. As your bird experiences more repetitions of the behavior and receives positive reinforcement, he will look forward to doing the behavior and have no motivation to be aggressive in that circumstance.

Frustration Aggression

Frustration is a state to which we can all relate. Most of us have experienced it while standing in long lines at the post office, watching an obnoxious customer get attention when we have been patient, and dealing with an automated answering service when we need a live person. What an uncomfortable state of mind! I am sure many of us have resorted to aggressive behavior once we have reached our limits. Aggressive for humans may be speaking with the manager, writing an angry letter, yelling at the salesperson, or pounding the buttons on the phone. For a parrot, one might observe lunging, aggressive grabbing of an object with the beak, charging, and biting. Some birds will also redirect aggression onto other objects in response to the frustration, such as ripping paper or biting at toys.

Frustration aggression is the result of an action being blocked. This can lead to a build up of aggression after a period of time in a certain circumstance. It is likely there are small signals occurring that could indicate the bird is beginning to become frustrated. We see that it is important for the person interacting with the bird to pay close attention to the bird's body language and take note of these signals. Those signals may indicate it is time to discontinue what is currently being done, or perhaps some positive reinforcement needs to be associated with this circumstance in order to change the bird's perception of the situation from frustration to pleasure.

A common scenario that is more frustrating for a bird than most people realize is when a bird is required to wait or sit still in a certain

Learned aggression is challenging to correct. Reinforcing an incompatible behavior, such as sitting quietly on a perch, is often the best method in this situation.

location for a period of time. It is so easy for us to forget to reinforce a bird that is sitting calmly. We also tend to forget that sitting still for a period of time is a behavior that is also achieved by gradually increasing the time a bird is required to sit. It is unreasonable to assume a bird will have motivation to sit still for a period of time unless we teach him to do so. Other bird species do this as well. For example; ground hornbills, crows, and ravens will pound on things with their beaks in frustration.

Over the years I have worked in a few shows that included ground hornbills, crows, and ravens. The birds in these shows had been trained to sit in large dog kennels or holding areas prior to their entrance onto the stage. The doors to the kennels and holding areas had been modified so that they were solid panels. Animals are incredibly perceptive and these birds all quickly learned a variety of things that signaled they were about to make their entrance and earn some treats on stage. They cued off of things such as the positions of various trainers, dialog, and the music in the show. A minute or two

Hornbills, such as this Jackson's hornbill, can exhibit aggressive behaviors as a result of frustration, similar to parrots. During a presentation given by the author, hornbills were inadvertently reinforced for knocking on doors as they waited for their portion of the show. This knocking behavior resulted from the bird's strong desire to perform and gain some tasty treats on stage.

before it was time to go on stage, the birds would pace as if they were quite anxious to get on with their parts in the show. Training with positive reinforcement creates a great deal of motivation! These intense desires to do their behaviors also lead to some intense pounding on the doors to the kennels and holding areas. In one show, we actually used the pounding to simulate a knock on the door, which cued the trainer to open the door and release the bird. In another show, we simply opened the door on the scripted cue. Because we were going by the cue in the script, we inadvertently reinforced the behavior of pounding every time we opened the door when the bird was pounding. The bird pounded at the door in frustration because he was anxious to get out on stage and receive his treats. We opened the door when he did this, therefore, the bird learned to keep pounding when he wanted to go on stage. For this show, the pounding occurred in areas that were far enough way from the audience that it did not disrupt the show.

This may not be the case in your home. If you notice something frustrates your bird, discontinue the cause of the frustration, try not to accidentally reinforce it, and think of what behavior you could train your bird to do that would allow it to avoid the frustrating circumstance. Use your knowledge of approximations to create a training strategy and focus on eliminating frustration by positively reinforcing good behavior in that situation.

Personal Aggression

Even though a bird may have a personal dislike for someone, it does not mean there is no hope of getting past the aggressive behavior. It does mean some work needs to be done to build a relationship built on positive experiences for the person in question and the bird. This is sometimes challenging because usually the person who is the target of this aggression is not all that interested in making friends with the Tasmanian devil disguised as a parrot. This is certainly understandable, but if the person wants to make the effort there are things that can be done.

The first step is to set the bird and the person up for success. This goes back to the guideline of avoiding aggression. Some things tend to contribute to heightened levels of aggression. For example, some birds are more aggressive in or around their cages. Some birds are also more aggressive if there is a person in the room that he or she prefers to the one in question. Another recommended guideline is to consider working in neutral territory. This can be very helpful in this situation. A bird that is aggressive around his cage, may become much more receptive to a person he has disliked in the past when both are in a place away from the cage. It will be important for the person interacting with the bird to be sensitive to any displays of aggression by the parrot and not push for too much. A great way to start building a relationship is to ask the bird to do a simple behavior he knows how to do very well. For example, the person may cue the bird to turn around or wave. This gives the bird somewhere to focus his attention, rather than on aggression. And it also gives the bird an opportunity to receive positive reinforcement for doing a behavior. This positive reinforcement is then directly associated with the person he has previously disliked. The person can cue the bird for behaviors as fast as he can eat the treats.

Every time the bird receives positive reinforcement from the person, it builds up a history of good experiences with the person.

I often compare this type of relationship to a balance scale. One side of the scale represents a history of positive experiences, the other side represents negative experiences associated with the person he dislikes. In the beginning the scale is tipped in favor of the negative experiences. In order to change the relationship, the person's job is to tip the scale in favor of the positive experiences. This can be done by avoiding anything that would cause the bird to be fearful or aggressive, and creating more experiences that the bird views as positive experiences with the new person. This scale concept can be applied to any behavior or situation that is challenging for your bird.

Specific Scenarios

The following are examples of aggressive behavior and how to address the problem using the strategies suggested in this book. Review the strategies again and see how they are used in these examples to provide a successful resolution to the problems presented. Notice how these strategies are used in the following scenarios to:

- Avoid circumstances that elicit aggressive behavior.
- Divert the attention.
- Not accidentally reinforce aggressive behavior if possible.
- Reinforce any behavior other than aggressive behavior.
- Teach cooperation with small approximations and positive reinforcement.
- Teach your bird to do behaviors that are incompatible with aggression.
- Reduce aggression through the repetition of a simple behavior.

Scenario 1:
Your bird climbs onto you shoulder and bites when you try to get him down.

If the behavior of climbing to your shoulder occurs often, this indicates the bird finds sitting on your shoulder reinforcing. If you do not want the bird to sit on your shoulder in the future, you can focus on training the bird to sit on your hand. One method that is quite effective involves using a hand position that makes sitting on the hand a preferred choice for the bird. This can be done by making the hand the most elevated point of your arm. Often when a bird begins to climb up towards the shoulders, people lower their hands to encourage the bird to climb down. This usually results in the opposite behavior. Most parrots prefer to sit in the most elevated, comfortable perch available. While your bird is sitting on your hand make a bend in your wrist and hold your forearm in a vertical position. This looks similar to a waiter holding a serving tray. This help makes your hand the most elevated perch. The vertical position of the forearm is challenging for the parrot to climb down. In addition, positive reinforcement in the form of treats, attention, toys can be offered to the bird for sitting on the hand. This strategy helps avoid the situation of having to deal with a bird that does not want to leave the shoulder.

If the bird is already sitting on the shoulder, it may be helpful to have another person cue the bird to step up onto his or her hand. Positively reinforce the bird for stepping up on the hand so that the bird will be likely to step up in the future.

If no other person is available, you can position your body near a perch or cage and allow the bird to step off the shoulder onto the perch or cage. Offer the bird positive reinforcement for stepping onto the perch or cage. Try to avoid forcing the bird onto the perch or cage.

Also, try to avoid prying the bird off your shoulder or chasing the bird with your hands. This strategy would be incorporating negative reinforcement and could lead to a bite. Instead, focus on teaching the bird to step up onto your hand reliably for positive reinforcement.

Scenario 2:
Your bird is in a kennel and tries to bite when you attempt to take him out.

Sometimes your bird may need to go into a kennel, for example, if you need to visit the veterinarian. However, at some point you will require the bird to exit the kennel. Because the bird chooses to stay in the kennel, this indicates there is reinforcing value to your bird to remain in the kennel. This may be because the bird views the kennel as a nest box and is demonstrating territorial type behavior. It may simply be that your bird likes the kennel, or finds the environment outside the

Parrots enjoy elevated perches, including shoulders. They may try to bite if forcibly removed. You can avoid this by raising your hand above your shoulder; your bird will probably move up to your hand.

kennel less comfortable. Because the bird is biting at the hand that reaches into the kennel, the best way to avoid aggression would be to avoid putting your hand in the kennel. Therefore, other strategies will be required to get the bird out without aggression.

Because parrots generally prefer to perch on the most elevated position, this can be used as positive reinforcement for the behavior of leaving the kennel. The kennel can be placed so that the door to the kennel is opened towards the ceiling. Usually parrots will voluntarily climb towards the opening to comfortably perch on the opened door outside of the kennel.

Another strategy is to teach the bird with shaping approximations and positive reinforcement that coming out of the kennel will result in things the bird likes. This can be initiated by making a small trail of favorite food items leading from the opening of the kennel. The bird can be allowed to come out on his own volition and eat the treats. Once the bird is outside of the kennel, the kennel can be removed so that the bird no longer has the opportunity to climb back into the kennel.

To solidify the behavior of leaving the kennel for the future, it is helpful to allow the bird to experience repetitions of going in and out of the kennel. Each time the bird leaves the kennel, positive reinforcement can follow. This will increase the likelihood the bird will leave the kennel more readily in the future.

Scenario 3:
You have a parrot that shows extremely aggressive behaviors whenever anybody is close to the cage.

More than likely this bird is demonstrating territorial aggression. Usually a bird such as this receives less and less attention and may learn to have fewer reasons to want to interact with people. Owners can work on developing the relationship by simply offering favorite food items whenever people are nearby to help create a situation in which the bird looks forward to the presence of people. Training a simple behavior such as targeting or walking from point A to point B can give the bird something on which he can focus his attention on instead of aggression. These behaviors can be trained without the need to handle the bird or even take the bird out of the cage. Repetitions of this behavior with different individuals allows the bird to associate positive reinforcement with different people while keeping his attention focused on the trained behavior.

If the goal is not necessarily to create a bird that will interact with people, but to avoid aggressive behaviors, the bird can be trained to shift or move into another area or enclosure if the cage needs to be accessed without the bird present. Some cages are available that include a shift door. This door can be opened to allow a bird to enter another enclosure. The door can be closed behind the bird to prevent the bird from returning to the original enclosure while it is being serviced. Teaching the bird to move to the other side can be done with positive reinforcement training. In some cases it is as simple as placing the bird's food bowl on the other side of the door. A bird can also be trained with positive reinforcement to go into a kennel or crate while the cage is serviced. This also allows aggressive encounters to be avoided.

Scenario 4:

When you take your bird to the veterinarian's office, your bird tries to bite the veterinarian.

Your bird may try to bite the veterinarian for many different reasons. One reason may be that your bird has learned to associate negative experiences with that person. Another reason may be that your bird has not had positive reinforcement associated with new people and new places. In other words, your bird has not been trained to be comfortable in that situation. In addition, your bird may simply not like what is being done at that moment.

One the easiest ways to prepare your bird for visits to the veterinarian is through positive reinforcement training. You can train your bird to voluntarily step up onto many different people with positive reinforcement as the consequence. Additionally, giving your bird the opportunity to experience new environments associated with positive reinforcement will enable your bird to be comfortable responding to cued behaviors such as step up in places he does not often

Many parrots display territorial aggression around their cages. You can avoid this by letting the bird come out on his own or by training him through positive reinforcement to accept people in his space.

visit. You can also train a variety of behaviors that may be helpful in the veterinary exam. These behaviors may include getting on a scale, allowing touch, allowing wings to be stretched out, going in and out of a kennel and much more.

Another training goal that can be helpful to establish before going to the veterinarian is teaching your bird to being comfortable wrapped in a towel. Playing in a towel and allowing a towel to be gently placed over your bird is an activity that can be practiced in the home. When at the veterinarian's office this same activity can be initiated by you, the parrot owner. Once the bird's head is gently covered by the towel, the veterinarian or technician can step in to gently apply restraint. Having the bird's head covered before actual restraint is applied helps avoid the bird associating the negative experience of the being restrained with any one individual. This in turn can help prevent aggressive behavior directed at a specific individual.

Scenario 5:

Your bird is out on his play stand. You need to leave for work. When you try to put him back in his cage, your bird refuses to step up onto your hand and is now trying to bite your hand when it is presented.

More than likely the bird's refusal to step up indicates that he enjoys spending time on his play stand. It is also possible that past experiences have taught the bird that stepping up from the play stand at that time of the day results in being locked in his cage and loss of pleasant interactions with you as you head off to work.

There are a variety of strategies that can be applied. If the time before going to work is constrained, it may be a good choice to leave the bird in the cage in the morning. Playtime can be reserved for times of the day when you do not need to quickly return the bird to the cage.

Another strategy is to focus on training the bird to step up from the play stand for positive reinforcement. This may take some time since the bird has now learned that stepping up may result in something he does not like. Therefore, the behavior of stepping up may need to be broken down into small approximations again and retrained with positive reinforcement. It is also helpful to ask the bird to step up on occasion and not return the bird to the cage every time. This will help the bird to not anticipate something negative following the step up behavior.

In addition to training step up, training the behavior of going back into the cage for positive reinforcement will be helpful. One suggestion is to place the bird's favorite food in the food bowl in the cage while the bird is on the play stand. When the bird is returned to the cage, there will be a large reinforcement of breakfast waiting in the cage.

If you are in a bind and need to return the bird to the cage and the bird will not step up, the perch upon which the bird is sitting can be carried over to the cage to allow the bird to step into his cage. There is no need to endure a bite to get the bird back in the cage. However this strategy can be avoided by focusing on using positive reinforcement to train the desired behavior.

Scenario 6:

Your bird is flighted and is bonded to you. Whenever your spouse enters the room, the bird launches a dive-bomb attack on your significant other.

Because the bird is bonded to you, more than likely the bird is flying after your spouse to drive him or her out of the perceived territory and away from you. This can be challenging to address because of the instinctual drive that tells the bird to do this. However, there are things that can be done to reduce the likelihood of an attack. One simple action is to not allow the bird out of the cage when you anticipate your spouse will be around. You can also warn your spouse the bird is outside of the cage by posting a sign or signal by the entryway to the room so that your spouse does not accidentally put him or herself into the situation. You can also identify times of the day when others are not around to be appropriate for outside the cage interactions.

Avoiding creating the situation in which the bird is likely to attack is usually the easiest strategy. It is possible to try to train the bird to be calm around your spouse. But this does take effort on the part of both you and your spouse. What is often difficult in this situation is that the spouse may not have an interest in trying to develop a relationship with a parrot that seems to be driven to attack him or her. However, if you do have a spouse willing to participate, you can try using positive reinforcement to help improve the relationship.

Usually it is easier to begin to develop a relationship away from the territory and away from the bird's perceived mate. This may mean you place the bird in a cage or perch in another room and then leave the room. Your spouse can then enter the room with a stash of treats. The treats can be offered simply for calm behavior. If the bird knows a simple behavior on cue, your spouse can cue the bird for this simple behavior over and over. If the bird is still displaying strong aggressive behaviors, treats can be dropped in a bowl or offered from a bowl or spoon to avoid placing fingers too close to the beak. Once progress is made without your presence, the training can include approximating you back into the scenario. Over time you can attempt to gradually enter the room while the bird is being reinforced for calm behavior. Any sign of aggression can cause you to leave the room. Again this strategy can take time and a willing partner. For some households, avoiding the situations that create aggressive behavior is the preferred choice.

When a parrot pair bonds to a person, he may decide to attack other people. This is a challenging behavior to correct.

Scenario 7:

You are playing catch with your parrot while he sits on top of his cage. He is very excited as he tosses the ball about. When you try to take the ball to toss it to him, he lunges for your hand.

In this situation it appears the activity of play has created a heightened level of excitement for your parrot. The type of play in which he was engaging became too intense for him. Rather than punish your bird, you can make note that this type of play activity can create some undesired behavior. You can avoid the aggressive behavior by discontinuing the interactive play when you observe this level of excitement. You can always return when the bird seems to have calmed down a bit.

You can also avoid the aggressive behavior by having other play alternatives. More than one ball may allow you to toss a ball to your bird without having to attempt to remove the first ball. You can also cue or redirect your bird to one side of the cage away from the ball and positively reinforce your bird for going in that direction. While the bird is away from the ball you can remove it and initiate the play behavior again.

You can also consider other interactive play that may not elevate your bird to that level of excitement.

Scenario 8:

Your bird is sitting on your shoulder and begins to destroy your favorite earrings. Pushing his beak away with your hands just seems to create an aggressive response.

Probably the most successful way of avoiding an encounter that might include aggressive behavior in this situation is to avoid wearing earrings when your bird is on your shoulder. Another option is to train your bird to sit someplace other than your shoulder if you would prefer to wear earrings and have your bird out.

Also successful is to give your bird a quick time-out the moment the bird begins to play with your earrings. This does require that your bird steps up reliably from you shoulder. After the bird steps up and a few seconds of time-out have passed, he can be allowed on the shoulder again. If the bird does not chew on your earrings, offer positive reinforcement for not chewing. If he does chew, another short time-out can be repeated. Quickly, the bird should learn that chewing results in a time-out. Sitting on the shoulder without chewing offers positive reinforcement.

If you have trained your bird to drop an item on cue, you can also cue the bird to drop the earring, and then follow this with positive reinforcement. Again prevention is very helpful to avoiding aggressive behavior in this situation.

Scenario 9:

Your bird has been screaming and it is driving you crazy. You run into the room and in, your agitated state, begin yelling at your bird. Your bird gets very excited as well and bites his own leg.

Screaming can become a behavioral problem when it gets reinforced. In this case running into the room and/or yelling may reinforce that behavior. However, the curious part is why your bird responded by biting his own leg. In this situation it is possible that the excitement created in the bird by your quick appearance and yelling may have created an act of redirected aggression.

The bird may have found your behavior unpleasant and responded by biting something nearby that he could access. The bird could also have found your response exciting and responded almost with an automatic reaction of biting something nearby. In any case, it was clear your behavior was the catalyst for the redirected aggression. By refraining from suddenly appearing and/or yelling at the bird, the redirected aggression can be avoided.

Scenario 10:

You are in the middle of a training session, and your bird starts chewing aggressively on the perch.

One question to ask yourself when this type of situation is observed is if the bird appears to be having difficulty understanding what it is you want him to do. If a bird is motivated to participate in a training session, he will often try very hard to earn the positive reinforcement. If during that session, nothing the bird tries seems to get him that positive reinforcement, displaced aggression such as chewing on the perch may be observed. In these situations it is helpful to use smaller approximations to help clearly communicate what it is you would like your bird to do. It also allows the bird to begin to receive some positive reinforcement. This helps to keep the bird motivated to participate and avoids the situation that might create frustration. Try to create the situation in which the approximations are small enough that your bird never has the opportunity to make a mistake. Each step or approximation takes the bird forward toward the desired behavior.

Scenario 11:
You have just acquired a bird, and you would like him to step up onto your hand. However, the moment he sees your hand coming towards him, he lunges for it.

I have saved this scenario for last because I hope people will remember the lesson learned here most of all. A bird that immediately lunges for a hand has probably been chased by hands at some point in his life. He has learned that trying to bite a hand will make that frightening hand go away. This situation happens when we try to use force to train a bird to get onto the hand. This type of behavior is often the result of applying the concept that a bird must obey the step up command.

If there is one training strategy I hope people learn to avoid it is the practice of forcing a bird to step up onto your hand. It is something that has been taught to the parrot community for many years. But it is, without a doubt, not necessary. Birds can easily be trained to step up onto the hand for positive reinforcement. This is especially easy when done with a young bird. However, once a bird has learned to fear hands, it becomes much more challenging. The result of this misinformation is that many, many birds have learned to bite hands. These birds are most likely destined to remain in cages only because someone used force to try to train that bird. Had positive reinforcement training been the choice from the beginning, the result may have been many more emotionally healthy birds and satisfying bird/owner relationships.

The beauty of training birds to step up for positive reinforcement is that the birds learn to trust that you will not do anything to them they do not like. In other words, you do not give them a reason to want to bite you. People sometimes say, "I don't mind if he bites" or "He wasn't trying to bite hard." For me, any thought about biting means I am doing something wrong. I personally never want to do anything that would cause a bird to even think he needs to bite me. I much prefer a calm, comfortable bird. And I know I can influence that greatly by the choices I make.

Positive reinforcement training allows the bird to choose to participate. If the bird chooses to participate, good things will happen. If the bird chooses not to participate, the only consequence is the loss of an opportunity to gain some treats or other positive reinforcement. This is very different from being chased around a cage, or pushed into a corner, or scooped up by hands covered in towels, etc.

It is challenging to train a bird that has already been exposed to negative reinforcement training or punishing strategies for the behavior of stepping up on the hand. But it is not impossible. As with the other aggression scenarios, it is best to avoid creating aggression. Therefore, putting your hand in the cage may not be a good choice. Instead work on luring the bird out of the cage with a treat. Allow the bird to choose to come out in a way that is comfortable for the bird. You can always

Past emphasis on making parrots step up on a finger on command has caused many birds to be frightened of and aggressive toward hands. You can teach you bird to enjoy stepping up by using positive reinforcement.

lure your bird back into his cage by putting favorite foods in his food bowl. He doesn't need to step up to go back in the cage. To begin training step up for positive reinforcement, place your hand in a stationary position away from the bird and positively reinforce the bird for calmly coming towards your hand. Over time you will teach your bird that your hand will not come after him. But, if your bird chooses to come to your hand, good things will happen, such as receiving favorite treats.

Eventually you can work to the point that your bird will voluntarily step onto your hand for positive reinforcement. It is extremely rewarding when a bird that has learned aggression toward hands successfully learns to step up for positive reinforcement. Usually it is the first step towards building a great relationship with a bird. It was not the bird's fault that his first exposure to hands was frightening and taught him to bite. Knowing that you can make a difference by choosing to apply kinder and gentler methods to get desired behavior can change the lives of companion parrots for the better.

Conclusion

At first, aggression may seem like one giant ball of yarn knotted up. But, as we pull at the threads we find the yarn is actually woven into a very clear and specific pattern. This pattern is the inner workings of aggression and is highlighted by the principles of behavior. It is quite organized, ready and waiting to be studied and understood. The real life examples I presented were based on my personal experiences working as an animal trainer. Many of the explanations of how aggression works are the result of the work of many researchers in the scientific community. Aggression is not a new subject, and people have many good reasons to want to understand how it works for a number of species, including humans.

If you want to learn more about aggression, I suggest you check the references and resources section of this book and continue expanding your understanding of aggression. You will find this knowledge useful in many areas of your life, not just when interacting with your companion parrot. This is one of the many fascinating benefits of exploring animal behavior. It often leads to many insights into our own behavior.

I also want to applaud those of you who have picked up this book in hopes of addressing the aggression issues you may have experienced with your parrot. Birds are small creatures, and often it can be easy to resort to unpleasant interactions in an attempt to gain cooperation. It is so exciting to see caring companion parrot owners seeking answers and methods to modify behavior that do not rely on punishment and aversives. The future of companion animal training is evolving for the better.

Over the years, many animal trainers have learned you can accomplish all your training goals and more by focusing on positive experiences for both the animal and trainer. I recently read an interview with Ken Ramirez, Director of Training at Shedd Aquarium, in which he stated the best trainers never have the word *no* as part of their vocabulary when working with an animal. What a strange concept for humans to grasp! He is absolutely right. You can train everything you would like without ever saying "no" to an animal, while at the same time maintaining good behavior. This twist in thinking may contradict some traditional methods of modifying behavior. However, when we consider dropping the word *no,* eliminating aversives, and avoiding aggression, we can begin the journey toward the most loving relationship possible with those beings in our lives.

Thank *you* for considering the kinder and gentler path to good behavior. I hope this journey into aggression has been enlightening.

All your training goals can be accomplished with positive interactions if you are conscientious and sensitive to your bird's body language.

Bibliography
and References

Archer, J. *The Behavioural Biology of Aggression*. Cambridge University Press, 1988.

Baenninger, Ronald. "Some Consequences of Aggressive Behavior: A Selective Review of the Literature on Other Animals." *Aggressive Behavior*. Vol. I, 17-37. 1974.

Chance, Paul. *Learning and Behavior*. Pacific Grove: Brooks/Cole Publishing Co., 1999.

Decaire, Michael W., HBSc. *Aggression Types and Criminal Behavior*. at www.uplink.com.au/lawlibrary/documents/docs/doc18.html

Dilger, W.C. "The Comparative Ethology of the African Parrot Genus *Agapornis*." *Z. Tierpsyhcol*. 17: 649-685. 1960.

Fisher, Roger and William Ury. *Getting Past No: Negotiating with Difficult People*. New York: Bantam, 1991.

Friedman, PhD., Susan G. and Bobbi Brinker. "The Facts about Punishment." *Original Flying Machine*. Issue 4: Jan/Feb. 2001.

Johnson, C.M. and K.S Norris. "Delphinid Social Organization and Social Behavior." *Dolphin Cognition and Behavior: A Comparative Approach*. 335-346. Hillsdale: Lawrence Carlbaum, 1986.

Kazdin, Alan E. *Behavior Modification in Applied Settings*. Fifth Edition. Pacific Grove: Brooks/Cole Publishing Co., 1994.

Kenyon, Paul, PhD. *Aggression: Study and Learning Materials On Line*. University of Plymouth. http://salmon.psy.plym.ac.uk/year2/aggression/aggression.html

Lacinak, T. and G. Priest. *Aggression Workshop*. Animal Behavior Management Alliance Annual Conference. Baltimore, MD.April, 2004

Lorenz, Konrad. *On Aggression*. New York: Harcourt, Brace & World, 1966.

Masello, Juan F. and Petra Quillfeldt. "Chick Growth and Breeding Success of the Burrowing Parrot." *Condor*. 104: 574-586. 2002.

Mazur, J. E. *Learning and Behavior*. Upper Saddle River: Prentice Hall, 2002.

Moyer, K.E. *The Psychology of Aggression*. New York: Harper and Row, 1976.

Pidgeon, R. "Calls of the Galah (*Cacatua roseicapilla*) and Some Comparisons With Four Other Species of Australian Parrots." *Emu*. 81:158-168. 1981

Ramirez, Ken. *Animal Training: Successful Animal Management Through Positive Reinforcement*. Chicago: Shedd Aquarium Press, 1999.

Saunders, D.A. "The Function and Displays in the Breeding of the White Tailed Black Cockatoo." *Emu*. 74: 43-46. 1974.

Selye, Hans. *The Stress of Life*. New York: McGraw-Hill, 1978, 1976.

Skinner, B.F. "The Behavior of Organisms: An Experimental Analysis." *The Century Psychology Series*. New York: Appleton-Century-Crofts, 1938.

Smith, K. Dorey, N., Morehead, M. & Rosales-Ruiz, J. "The effects of the immediate presentation of a conditioned reinforcer and the delayed presentation of food on the behavior of sheep." In N. Dorey (Chair). "Tales from the zoo: Some relevant variables to target training." Symposium conducted at the 29th International Meeting of the Association for Behavior Analysis. San Francisco, CA., May 2003.

Snyder, N.F.R., J.W. Wiley and C.B. Kepler. *The Parrots of Luquillo: Natural History and Conservation of the Puerto Rican Parrot.* Los Angeles: The Western Foundation of Vertebrate Zoology, 1987.

Turner, T. and C. Tompkins. "Aggression: Exploring the Causes and Possible Reduction Techniques." *International Marine Animal Training Association Soundings.* Vol.15 No 2. 1990.

Wickler, W. "Vocal Dueting and the Pair Bond: Coyness and Partner Commitment: a Hypothesis." *Z. Tierpsychol.* 52: 201-209. 1980.

Wickler, W. and U. Seibt. "Vocal Dueting and the Pair Bond: II Unison Dueting in the African Forest Weaver (*Symplectes bicolor*)." *Z. Tierpsychol.* 52:217-226. 1980.

Resources

Organizations

American Federation of Aviculture
P.O. Box 7312
N. Kansas City, MO 64116
Telephone: (816) 421-2473
Fax: (816) 421-3214
E-mail: afaoffice@aol.com
http://www.afabirds.org/

Avicultural Society of America
P.O. Box 5516
Riverside, CA 92517-5516
Telephone: (951) 780-4102
Fax: (951) 789-9366
E-mail: info@asabirds.org
http://www.asabirds.org/index.php

Aviculture Society of the United Kingdom
Arcadia-The Mounts-East Allington-Totnes
Devon TQ9 7QJ
United Kingdom
E-mail: admin@avisoc.co.uk
http://www.avisoc.co.uk/

British Bird Council
1st Floor Offices
1159 Bristol Road South
Northfield, Birmingham, B31 2SL
Telephone: 01214-765999
http://www.britishbirdcouncil.com/

The International Association of Avian Trainers and Educators
350 St. Andrews Fairway
Memphis, TN 38111
Telephone: (901) 685-9122
Fax: (901) 685-7233
E-mail: secretary@iaate.org
www.IAATE.org

The Parrot Society of Australia
P.O. Box 75
Salisbury, Queensland 4107
Australia
E-mail: petbird@parrotsociety.org.au
http: //www.parrotsociety.org.au

Publications
Bird Talk Magazine
3 Burroughs
Irvine, CA 92618
Telephone: (949) 855-8822
Fax: (949) 855-3045
http://www.birdtalkmagazine.com/bt/

Bird Times Magazine
7-L Dundas Circle
Greensboro, NC 27407
Telephone: (336) 292-4047
Fax: (336) 292-4272
E-mail: info@petpublishing.com
www.birdtimes.com

Good Bird Magazine (published by the author)
PO Box 684394
Austin, TX 78768
Telephone: 512-423-7734
Fax: 512-236-0531
Email: info@goodbirdinc.com
http://www.GoodBirdInc.com

Parrots Magazine (UK)
Imax Ltd.
12 Riverside Business Centre
Brighton Road, Shoreham-by-Sea,
BN43 6RE
Telephone: 01273 464 777
Fax: 01273 463 999
E-Mail: info@imaxweb.co.uk
www.parrotmag.com

Parrots Magazine (USA)
P.O. Box 386
Goleta, CA 93116
Telephone: (800) 294-7951
Fax: (978) 246-7951
www.parrotmag.com

Internet Resources
The Animal Behavior Management Alliance
www.TheABMA.org

Applied Companion Animal Behavior Network- Avian Pages
Email: info@acabn.com
www.acabn.com/avianlist.html

Behavior Works
www.Behaviorworks.org
This is the site of Susan Friedman, PhD. It provides information on the online class Living and Learning with Parrots and also a link to the writings of Dr. Friedman.

An Animal Trainers Introduction to Operant and Classical Conditioning
www.wagntrain.com/OC.
This site attempts to explain operant conditioning, and promote the use of positive reinforcement and negative punishment in animal training.
Behavior Logic
www.behaviorlogic.com
Online magazine about learning and behavior.

BirdCLICK
(www.geocities.com/Heartland/Acres/9154/)
A site and e-mail list devoted to clicker training pet birds.

Clicking with Birds
www.clickingwithbirds.com
Learn the basics of positive reinforcement training with Linda Morrow.

Exotic Pet Vet.Net
(http://www.exoticpetvet.net)
This website, authored by an avian veterinarian and an aviculturist/zoologist, offers extensive information on a variety of bird-related topics, including nutrition, health, and emergency care.

HolisticBird.org
(http://www.holisticbird.org)
HolisicBird.org maintains that the mental, emotional, and spiritual wellness of a bird's whole being is directly tied to health. With this belief in mind, HolisticBird.org provides information on diet, nutrition, healing, and behavior from a holistic perspective.

The Parrot Pages
(http://www.parrotpages.com)
This site is a prime source for avian information including links to conservation and research centers, and international parrot breeders and avian suppliers.

Vet Talk: The Bird Hotline
(www.birdhotline.com/vet.htm)
This interactive site allows avian-loving individuals to post inquiries to a veterinarian certified in Avian Practice via the Internet.

Veterinary Resources
Association of Avian Veterinarians (AAV)
P.O. Box 811720
Boca Raton, FL 33481-1720
Telephone: (561) 393-8901
Fax: (561) 393-8902
E-mail: AAVCTRLOFC@aol.com
http://www.aav.org/

Emergency Resources and Rescue Organizations
ASPCA Animal Poison Control Center
Telephone: (888) 426-4435
E-mail: napcc@aspca.org (for non-emergency, general information only)
http://www.apcc.aspca.org

Austin Avian Rescue and Rehabilitation
8647 Highway 290 W
Austin, TX 78736
Phone: 512-288-2199
Fax: 512-288-3506
http://www.jandmaviariesinc.com

Bird Hotline
P.O. Box 1411
Sedona, AZ 86339-1411
E-mail: birdhotline@birdhotline.com
http://www.birdhotline.com/

The Gabriel Foundation
1025 Acoma Street
Denver, CO 80204
Telephone: (970) 963-2620
Fax: (970) 963-2218
E-mail: gabriel@thegabrielfoundation.org
http://www.thegabrielfoundation.org
A nonprofit corporation promoting education, conservation, rescue,
rehabilitation, adoption, and sanctuary for the needs of parrots everywhere.

National Parrot Rescue and Preservation Foundation (NPRPF)
5116 Bissonnet #471
Bellaire, TX 77401
www.parrotfestival.org
Parrot Education and Adoption Center PEAC
P.O. Box 600423
San Diego, CA 92160
E-mail: parroted@cox.net
www.PEAC.org

Parrot Rehabilitation Society
P.O. Box 620213
San Diego, CA 92102
www.parrotsociety.org

RSPCA
Wilberforce Way
Southwater
Horsham, West Sussex RH13 9RS
Telephone: 0870 3335 999
www.rspca.org.uk

RSPCA Australia
P.O. Box 265
Deakin West ACT 2600
Telephone: 02 6283 8300
www.rspca.org.au

Bird Clubs and Societies
African Parrot Society
P.O. Box 204
Clarinda, IA 51632
http://www.wingscc.com/aps/

Asiatic Parrot Association
734 S. Boulder Hwy. Suite 400
Henderson, NV 89015

Avicultural Society
P.O. Box 47
Edenbridge, Kent TN8 7WP
E-mail: lee.palm@virgin.net
National Parrot Association
8 N. Hoffman Lane
Hauppage, NY 11788
Telephone: (516) 366-3562
Parrot Pen Pals
39 Ingleby Way
Wallington, Surrey SM6 9LP

South London, Surrey & Sussex Area Parrot Society
The Nutfield Memorial Hall
Nutfield, Redhill, Surrey RH1 4EL
Telephone: 01494 875641

The Aloha Parrot Association
P.O. Box 893519
Mililani, Hawaii 96789
Telephone: (808) 834-5676
www.AlohaParrot.com

The Long Island Parrot Society
P O Box 2754
North Babylon, NY 11703
Telephone: (631) 957-1100
www.liparrots.org

The National Council for Aviculture UK
4 Haven Crescent
Werrington, Stoke on Trent, Staffs ST9 0EY
Telephone: 01782 305042

The Parrot Society UK
Boreham, Nr Chelmsford CM3 3EF
Telephone: 01375 679868

The Parrot Society UK
Antler Club
Marlfeet Lane, Hull HU9 5AQ
Telephone: 01482 376833

Conservation Organizations
Loro Parque Foundation
www.loroparque-fundacion.org

Save the Parrots
www.savetheparrots.com

Kakapo Recovery Programme
www.kakaporecovery.org

World Parrot Trust (UK)
Glarmor House
Hayle, Cornwall TR27 4HB
Telephone: 44 01736 751 026
Fax: 44 01736 751 028
Email: uk@worldparrottrust.org

World Parrot Trust (USA)
P.O. Box 353
Stillwater, MN 55802
Telephone: (651) 275-1877
Fax: (651) 275-1891
Email: usa@worldparrottrust.org
www.worldparrottrust.org

Glossary

aggression: offensive or defensive behavior in response to aversive stimuli. For a parrot, this can include lunging, biting, and other more subtle body language.

anthropomorphism: applying human emotions or feeling to animals. For example, saying an animal is angry or mean would be anthropomorphic. Describing the behavior an animal is exhibiting (lunging, biting, etc.) avoids anthropomorphism. Avoiding being anthropomorphic allows one to focus on things that can be done to address the behaviors that are observed.

applied behavior analysis: a science that focuses on the attempt to solve behavior problems by providing antecedents and/or consequences that change behavior. Interventions based on operant conditioning usually focus directly on overt behavior in settings of everyday life and on the environmental events before, after, and during the behavior that can be used to achieve behavior change. This also includes understanding how learning occurs.

approximations: breaking down a desired behavior into small steps or parts. Each step must be learned before moving on to the next step. Eventually, all the steps together lead up to the final desired behavior. Approximations are used to train desired behavior by shaping the behavior.

aversive stimulus: a kind of stimulus that is considered unpleasant or painful by the subject. An aversive stimulus can decrease the probability of responding or can be reinforcing when removed. It is sometimes called a punisher or negative reinforcer.

baiting: (see bribing)

bribing: showing the subject the positive reinforcement (treat or reward) he will receive prior to and/or while performing the behavior. The liability of bribing is that the subject may decide the bribe is not sufficient to perform the behavior. Also known as luring or baiting.

bridge (bridging stimulus): a sound or signal that the subject has learned that means the behavior has been performed correctly and positive reinforcement will be presented. It is called a "bridge" because it bridges the gap in time between when the behavior was performed and when the subject will receive the positive reinforcement. An effective bridge should be easily distinguished from other sights and sounds the subject may experience. Some bridges commonly used by animal trainers include the word "good," a whistle, and a clicker.

capturing: training a behavior by reinforcing an animal in the act of doing the desired behavior. In capturing, the desired behavior is not created by teaching small approximations. The animal presents the completed behavior and is reinforced for it. For example, training a chicken to scratch on cue would be a behavior that can be easily trained by capturing.

classical conditioning: the process whereby a new or neutral stimulus is paired with a stimulus that can elicit a reflex response. Eventually, the subject can learn to present the reflex response upon the presentation of the new or neutral stimulus. This was pioneered by the research of Pavlov. In his research, he noted dogs learned to salivate in response to cues other than just the presentation of food.

clicker training: training in which the sound of the clicker is used as the bridge. Some people prefer using a clicker as a bridge because the sound is very distinct and sounds the same every time. It can be a very clear signal to the subject.

cue: a sound or signal that tells the subject what to do.

desensitize: the process of allowing the subject to become more comfortable with an object, person, and/or situation over time that previously produced a negative response.

differential reinforcement of incompatible behavior: this refers to reinforcing any behavior that directly interferes and cannot be performed with the undesired behavior. The incompatible behavior is often the direct opposite of the undesired behavior.

differential reinforcement of other behavior: this refers to a procedure in which a reinforcer follows any behavior the animal emits except a particular one. The result of this type of selective reinforcement can be a decrease in the frequency of an undesired behavior.

dominate: overpowering a subject physically or mentally in order to exert control over the subject.

ethology: an area of biology concerned with the analysis of the behavior patterns that evolve in natural habitats, either in species or in individual organisms, with particular emphasis on those patterns that do not depend on, or are not known to depend on, prior operant selection or respondent conditioning.

ethogram: a record of behavioral activity of an animal(s) in the wild.

extinguishing a behavior: refers to a procedure in which reinforcement of a previously reinforced behavior is discontinued. The usual and most prominent effect of extinction is to decrease the frequency of a performance.

extinction burst: excessive and often powerful performance of a previously positively reinforced behavior in order to gain reinforcement. It occurs just prior to the extinction of the behavior.

eye pinning: condition in which the pupils of a parrot dilate and restrict to tiny black dots. This displays a great deal of the colorful iris in some parrot species.

hard-wired behavior: (See instinct)

height dominance: controversial theory that parrots establish a dominance hierarchy based on the height at which they perch. Parrots that perch higher are said to be dominant. Opponents believe height dominance in parrots does not exist; instead parrots perch higher for the opportunity of better visibility, better lift for flight, comfort, etc.

howdying: the process of allowing two animals to acclimate to each other without the ability to harm each other through physical contact. It is a process often used in zoos to introduce new individuals to one another gradually.

innate: (see instinct)

instinct: behavior that does not need to be learned. It is believed to have a genetic component. Also known as hard-wired behavior, innate, or species-specific behavior. Some examples in birds include nest building, predator avoidance behaviors, and courtship.

Lorenz, K: an Austrian zoologist and ethologist. For his work in establishing the science of ethology, particularly his studies concerning the organization of individual and group behavior patterns, Lorenz was awarded the Nobel Prize for Physiology and Medicine in 1973. He derived his insights into behavior from studying fish and birds. With Oscar Heinroth, he discovered imprinting, an especially rapid and relatively irreversible learning process that occurs early in the individual's life. A central concept complementary to imprinting is the innate release mechanism, whereby organisms are genetically predisposed to be especially responsive to certain stimuli. Parts of his work have been quite controversial, especially his assertion that aggressive impulses are to a degree innate, and also his drawing of analogies between human and animal behavior.

luring: (see bribing)

modeling: observational learning that occurs when an animal observes another animal (the model) engage in a particular behavior. The observer sees the model perform the behavior, but does not receive any of the consequences of the model performing the behavior. The observer merely learns the behavior by watching the model.

motivation: desire or drive; the reason for a given behavior.

negative reinforcement: the removal of a stimulus following a behavior that serves to maintain or increase the frequency of the behavior. Another name for negative reinforcement is escape/avoidance training. Negative reinforcers tend to be aversive or unpleasant stimuli. To avoid negative reinforcers, learners often only work to the level necessary to accomplish this goal.

neutral location: any area that the subject does not consider part of his territory.

operant conditioning: an element of applied behavior analysis that focuses on how subjects learn. It involves a stimulus or antecedent, followed by the performance of a behavior, followed by a consequence. The consequence determines whether the behavior will be repeated or not. Negative reinforcement, positive reinforcement, and punishment are all elements of operant conditioning.

pair bond: a situation that naturally occurs between two parrots in the wild, often with a mate. Two parrots will intentionally spend most of their time together. A bonded pair may exhibit any or all of the following behavior: preen each other, regurgitate for each other, fly in synchronicity, sit side by side, behave aggressively towards other birds of the same species, and more. This bond can be shared with a human instead of a bird in captive situations. This is very likely to occur with a hand-raised parrot that spends the majority of his time with one person.

pin feather: when a feather is growing it appears to have a paper-like, opaque wrapper around it called a horny sheath. This is normal and is typically preened off by the parrot or his mate or the companion parrot owner. While the sheath is still on the feather, the feather is known as a pin feather.

positive reinforcement: the presentation of a stimulus following a behavior that serves to maintain or increase the frequency of the behavior. Another name for positive reinforcement is reward training. Positive reinforcers tend to be valued or pleasant stimuli. To get positive reinforcers, learners often enthusiastically exceed the minimum effort necessary to gain them.

Psittaciformes: scientific order of birds that specifies parrots. This group includes all parrot species (cockatoos, macaws, conures, parrots, parakeets, lorikeets, etc.).

punishment: the presentation of an aversive stimulus or removal of a positive reinforcer that serves to decrease or suppress the frequency of the behavior. The use of punishment tends to produce detrimental side effects, such as counter aggression, escape behavior, apathy, and fear. Also, punishment doesn't teach the learner how to earn positive reinforcement.

redirected aggression: the action of performing aggressive behavior on or towards anything other than the stimulus that is causing the aggression.

roosting: the act of a bird choosing a location and settling into that location to sleep for the night.

shaping: the use of approximations and positive reinforcement to create a desired behavior.

Skinner, B.F.: famous American psychologist noted for his contributions to the study of the learning process. He proposed that learning is a function of change in overt behavior. Changes in behavior are the result of an individual's response to events that occur in the environment. A response produces a consequence such as defining a word, hitting a ball, or solving a math problem. When a particular stimulus-response pattern is reinforced, the individual is conditioned to respond.

target: a tool that can be used to help shape behavior. Almost anything can be a target. Typically a subject is trained to go to or follow a target by associating positive reinforcement with the target. Example: A dog may follow his food bowl because he has received positive reinforcement (food) in the bowl.

teaching: method of communicating to change behavior. By applying certain communication techniques, the subject can learn what the desired response is. Teaching can be intentional or unintentional. Synonymous with training.

territorial aggression: aggressive behavior that occurs in conjunction with an area, object, or person that is perceived to be part of the bird's territory, such as the cage or food bowls.

territorial behavior: behavior that indicates a particular area, object, or person is exclusive to that individual bird. It appears to be innate or hard-wired behavior for parrots to establish an area that is to be used exclusively by that parrot and his mate.

time-out: temporarily ending a training session or removing the opportunity for the subject to perform behavior and receive positive reinforcement. By definition, it is a form of punishment.

training: method of communicating to change behavior. By applying certain communication techniques, the subject can learn what the desired response is. Synonymous with teaching.

Index

Photo Credits:

Larry Allen: 12, 14, 35, 48

Isabelle Francais: 20, 24, 108, 109, 157

Bonnie Jay: 32

Bobbye Land: 98, 143

Leslie Leddo: 11, 38

TFH Archives: 66, 146, 159, 166

John Tyson: 113

All other photographs by the author.

About the Author

Barbara Heidenreich has been a professional in the field of animal training since 1990. After receiving her degree from the University of California at Davis in zoology, she began her career training animals in zoological facilities. Her area of expertise is free-flight bird programs. She also specializes in training animals for conservation education programming and training behaviors that can benefit the health and welfare of animals. Her experience includes consulting on animal behavior and training in zoos around the world. She has extensive experience teaching animal training workshops, and regularly speaks at conferences, bird club meetings, and other animal related events.

Barbara is, at the time of this writing, President of the International Association of Avian Trainers and Educators (www.IAATE.org), a long time professional member of the American Association of Zoos and Aquarium (www.AZA.org), a professional member of The Animal Behavior Management Alliance (www.TheABMA.org), and an associate member of the International Marine Animal Training Association (www.IMATA.org). She currently operates her own business that specializes in animal training consulting with zoos, nature centers and the companion parrot community. Visit her websites at Animal Training and Consulting Services (www.ATandCS.com) and Good Bird Inc. (www.GoodBirdInc.com).

The author and her companion parrot of 17 years, Tarah, a blue-fronted Amazon.

Other publications by Barbara Heidenreich

Good Bird! A Guide to Solving Behavior Problems in Companion Parrots. (2004) Avian Publications, Minneapolis, MN.